AF559640

WHO GETS ELECTED

WHO GETS ELECTED

How and **Why**

PRADEEP GUPTA

RUPA

Published by
Rupa Publications India Pvt. Ltd 2023
7/16, Ansari Road, Daryaganj
New Delhi 110002

Sales centres:
Prayagraj Bengaluru Chennai
Hyderabad Jaipur Kathmandu
Kolkata Mumbai

Copyright © Pradeep Gupta 2023

The views and opinions expressed in this book are the author's own and the facts are as reported by him which have been verified to the extent possible, and the publishers are not in any way liable for the same.

All rights reserved.
No part of this publication may be reproduced, transmitted, or stored in a retrieval system, in any form or by any means, electronic, mechanical, photocopying, recording or otherwise, without the prior permission of the publisher.

P-ISBN: 978-93-5702-172-2
E-ISBN: 978-93-5702-182-1

First impression 2023

10 9 8 7 6 5 4 3 2 1

The moral right of the author has been asserted.

Printed in India

This book is sold subject to the condition that it shall not, by way of trade or otherwise, be lent, resold, hired out, or otherwise circulated, without the publisher's prior consent, in any form of binding or cover other than that in which it is published.

CONTENTS

INTRODUCTION

I have often said that politics is a science that is driven, at its core, by a combination of understanding human behaviour and its systems. At the heart of it, human behaviour is shaped by needs and aspirations. People's needs and their desires will, in turn, affect the choices they make in life. This is what drives politics as well. Voters make choices about whom to vote for, based on their needs and aspirations and who they believe will be the best fit to fulfil those needs, and thereby help them meet those aspirations.

Similarly, politicians act in ways that help them fulfil their own needs and desires. Such principles, being simple to comprehend, are what politics is all about. But often, these simple ideas are neglected in our understanding of politics. This book is meant to correct that neglect and plug the gaps in our understanding of how politics works.

This book has been written from and based on the wisdom I have gleaned from the many years of experience conducting exit polls. They reflect my experiences of being among voters and surveying their brush with governance, as well as through close interactions with politicians and understanding what drives them. But most of all, this book has been built through the experience of my own life and the journey that I have traversed.

This journey has not been easy, especially with the diversity within the country. In 2019, the country had eight national political parties, over 50 recognized regional parties and around 2,000 smaller, unrecognized parties. The country has diversity in different aspects—from geography (arid deserts and tropical forests to the Himalaya and the flood plains) to language (over 23 official languages and over 1,000 dialects, with the second-highest number of English speakers globally but within less than 10 per cent of the country's population). There is diversity in demography as well, with over 30 per cent of the population living in 6,000 cities, while the rest are scattered over 600,000 villages of varying sizes.

To get election forecasting right in a country of such scale and diversity can be extremely challenging. In May 2019, when the country saw the general elections, we reached out to over 800,000 people across the country and interviewed them to understand which way the political pendulum would swing. The effort was worth it as we managed to predict the elections spot-on. This wasn't an exception—we have managed to accurately forecast 56 of 60 elections so far.

I established Axis My India (AMI) as a printing and contract publishing company in April 1998, after having spent many years working with publications such as *India Today*, as well as advertising agencies, handling responsibilities ranging from printing to advertising.

In 2013, we started venturing into marketing and consumer research, and gradually into election forecasting. None of these came easy. At that point, polling agencies that were already in the business would partner with media organizations like television channels, newspapers or magazines in order to get a wider reach. However, when we first started, there were no takers for our work. No one in the media industry was ready to invest their faith in us, as we had no work experience. So, we decided to take the setback as a challenge to showcase our mettle.

There were four big assembly elections coming up that year—in Chhattisgarh, Madhya Pradesh, Rajasthan and Delhi. We decided to dive deep and conduct detailed pre-poll and post-poll surveys in each one of them. Through comprehensive and repeated surveys, we gathered post-poll forecasts for each of these states and the National Capital Territory of Delhi. But we had no particular media channel through which we could showcase the results. So, the question before us was: Even though we had done the hard work, how do we tell the world what we had found?

I have never believed in glamourizing our work but instead focussing on the task at hand. So, we simply announced our findings on our website and on my personal Facebook page. In three of the four states that went to the polls, we came the closest to predicting the exact results. In Madhya Pradesh, we predicted 162 seats for the Bharatiya Janata Party (BJP), and it got 162; we gave 60 seats to the Congress, and it won 58. In Chhattisgarh, we predicted 48 seats for the BJP and it got 49; similarly, we forecasted 38 for the Congress and it got 39 seats. In Delhi, we predicted 27 seats for the Aam Aadmi Party (AAP), and it won 28. Without having to shout from the rooftops, our predictions had announced for us that we were here—and we were here to stay.

Soon, my phone lines started buzzing, with media houses seeking to do exclusive tie-ups with me for the upcoming general elections in 2014. Election forecasting is a bit like cricket—there is no room for complacency and each ball is a new one. Although we get stronger with each election, each poll feels like a new test. In 2015, two years after we had started forecasting, a trial by fire came our way.

The Bihar elections of 2015 were on the horizon. The state had seen massive political churning, with arch-rivals Nitish Kumar and Lalu Prasad Yadav tying up and forming the Mahagathbandhan (MGB) or the Grand Alliance. A resurgent BJP, following Modi's and the party's thumping victories, was raring to repeat the performance.

After the voting got completed on 5 November, all our rival polling agencies released their predictions. We were expected to release ours as well, and we did. Our findings indicated that the MGB was going to win by a massive majority. Many others had predicted the opposite. Media organizations, which had promised to broadcast our findings, suddenly developed cold feet. They felt that we had made a mistake in our surveys and analyses. But I remained steadfast in my belief that we were right.

I had done my due diligence and re-verified the entire process before reaching the conclusion. So, when the media refused to showcase our results, we sent our forecasts to all the media houses as a press release. Two days later, when the results were announced, we were proved right. We had predicted 169–183 seats for the MGB, and it had bagged 178.

None of our accuracies have happened by chance. Every detail that goes into each step of election forecasting—from hiring field researchers to planning surveys and executing them, to analysing the results and minimizing errors—is worked upon and accounted for.

Our hiring process, for instance, is quite intensive: We look for surveyors for every language and dialect. We look for specific traits, from the surveyors being good listeners to their coming from less-privileged backgrounds (which would make it easier for them to connect with respondents in rural areas), to their having close to no vices. Our surveyors go through gruelling living conditions to be able to accurately collect data around voters and their preferences—for instance, they have to often spend nights in villages or small towns with no accommodation facilities. Surveyors have long days, where they often don't even have a proper break for lunch.

Even the routes they take are planned well in advance so that delays are minimized and their travel is efficient. While a lot of work goes into the preparation of questionnaires the surveyors carry with them for getting answers, a lot also goes into getting the right regional translations for these questionnaires. Before finalizing, our analysts and experts go to each state and travel with the survey team, where they consult local language experts to ensure that the language used in the questionnaires is lucid and free from bias.

As much as we trust our survey team, we have in-built checks and balances in place to ensure that nothing is left to chance with these surveys. For instance, every interview is recorded and then sent to quality auditors who scrutinize the recordings. On an average, the auditors randomly select and scrutinize 20 per cent of the interviews. The auditors score interviews for quality, on a metric that we have developed. If the interview does not score well, we deem it invalid. That is not the end of it. The work done by the auditors is, thereafter, scrutinized and reviewed by 'super checkers'.

Underlined in the stringent process is my firm belief that

we are not just in the business of exit polls. We are in the business of 'exact' polls. Quality and truthfulness are the biggest priorities for AMI, and there is no room for compromise on this, no matter how high the stakes or the pressure.

In October 2019, a day after Haryana had finished polling in the assembly elections, we were supposed to be out with the exit poll results the previous evening. However, our results were saying something in contradiction to the other exit polls. As against their findings that the BJP was getting re-elected smoothly, we had found that the going was tough for the party, and it was unlikely to gain a majority on its own. Instead, Haryana could see a coalition government taking power. I went on air on *India Today* and explained that we needed one more day before we declared the results.

This was an unusual announcement, because we had always been on time in declaring our findings. But in that one extra day, I wanted to review my team's report one more time. My team had surveyed more than 59,000 voters across 658 towns and villages of Haryana. In that one day, we deployed seven fresh teams to survey 4,000 more post-poll surveys. Having reviewed these fresh data, I was convinced that we could not be wrong. The next day, I went on air and declared what we had found. When the results came out, we stood vindicated. We had got it, as they say, bang on.

Growing up, my childhood was, unwittingly, the perfect initiation for me in every way possible. My grandfather was the one who had taken me to my first-ever political rally. My father, Motilal Gupta, took the initiation a bit further. He was a freedom fighter, and having worked closely with Mahatma Gandhi, was a man of ethics and strong political opinions. He would work together with politicians, from parliamentarians to legislators and councillors, as their political advisor. He would even help them design election campaigns—my passion has, in part at least, been a direct inheritance of this. My interest in politics piqued thanks to his wide circle of friends and followers, as well as due to his work in helping politicians succeed.

There was another part of my childhood that shaped me for what lay ahead. My childhood was one of traversing a great, long journey—a journey of the not-so-proverbial riches to rags. When I was born, my family was doing exceedingly well financially. We were possibly the only family in the area to have a car and a telephone in those years. But slowly, the prosperity waned and gave way to very hard times.

Growing up, there was not a week when I did not have to go to the market to sell copper and brass vessels that our family owned, so that we could have enough food to eat. When I went to study in Jabalpur, I would have barely enough money to pay my fees. I remember a time when I did not have money to pay for my mess fees in my hostel, so I simply just handed over my wristwatch to the mess authorities.

When the college took us students on a trip to Mumbai (then Bombay), we went to Juhu Beach and my friends decided to get coconut water, an iconic drink in those days associated with Mumbai and its beaches, especially. My friends wanted to take a photo of all of us, sipping on our coconuts on the beach. I had no money to buy a coconut, which might have cost, maybe, five rupees or so back then. So, I picked up an empty coconut from the beach and posed for the photo.

When I started earning, I was the only male earning family member who had to support 14 women at home—from my wife to my grandmother, my sister, my sister-in-law and her daughters. They were spread across in age groups—from 14 to 80. Living with them, understanding their needs and meeting their expectations taught me about human psychology a lot more than any formal education could possibly have.

All these hardships conditioned me to work relentlessly and come to the realization that what is important is not the money but the work that you put in. As a result, setbacks don't deter me. Instead, they have pushed me to work harder and ensure that I, and now AMI, get better at what we do.

These early experiences in politics, the early struggles, my insights into human psychology and my knack for number-crunching, have all gradually led me to what I do today—political consultancy and election forecasting.

But at the core of all I do, at its heart, are people—from my surveyors and voters to politicians and bureaucrats. This book is an effort to make you, the reader and the voter, understand just how people drive India's democracy. You don't need to be a Chanakya to understand or win elections, or predict elections fairly accurately, in this country. You just need to be able to understand people better.

This book, I hope, will help you do just that.

1

HOW NEEDS DRIVE DEMOCRACY

The three pivots of electoral politics in a democratic system are voters, politicians and governance. At the core of this system are the people, and lying at the heart of this democratic process are the needs of those people, i.e., the voters.

The needs of the voters, and whether they are fulfilled or not, shapes the fortunes of all the three pivots—the voters themselves, the politicians and the governance structures. Voters look towards the democratic process to meet their needs. What this means is that voters support politicians who have either addressed their needs or have the capacity to do so. A voter may have a few or many choices when it comes to backing a candidate or a political party while casting the ballot, but these choices are always determined by their needs—whether fulfilled or yet to be met.

The seminal rational choice theory,[1] which applies to various disciplines like economics and psychology, echoes this approach. Individuals take rational decisions with the aim of

---

[1]Ruhl, Charlotte, 'Introduction to Rational Choice Theory', *Simply Sociology*, 22 January 2022, https://bit.ly/3YzcxfV. Accessed on 14 February 2023.

maximizing their benefits. In the political sphere, it translates into the fact that the choice voters make in electing their representatives is based on their assessment of who can and will fulfil their needs the best.

But this fulfilment of needs is a complicated process because the question is not just about an individual need alone. It is about the needs of an entire ecosystem of the people. A voter is an individual, but he has a family, a circle of friends and relatives. They will all have a melange of needs, and not all of them would be common.

For instance, after the second wave of COVID-19, when thousands died across the country amidst a crippling shortage of everything—from hospital beds to oxygen—questions were asked on the impact that the crisis would have on the forthcoming elections in some states. But in the Uttar Pradesh elections held in May 2022, even families of those who died due to government negligence voted the ruling party, BJP, back to power. Various news reports pointed to this trend.[2] Many of these voters agreed that the government had not delivered during the second wave, but they argued that the government had delivered elsewhere—for some, the government had made them feel safer; for others, it had delivered welfare benefits. As a result, the ruling BJP was re-elected with a thumping majority.

The fact that the fundamental element of any free electoral system is the way that people make choices, and that those choices are dependent on the needs met and unmet, leads

---

[2]Khan, Fatima, 'Why Many Who Lost Loved Ones to COVID-19 Second Wave Are Still Voting for BJP', *The Quint*, 21 February 2022, https://bit.ly/3Rsh01h. Accessed on 2 February 2023.

one to examine the concept of needs more intimately and carefully. Most political analysts ignore the role 'needs' play in the election system in the belief that it is too 'psychological' and 'abstract' to actually determine the outcome. They could not be more wrong.

The noted twentieth-century social psychologist Abraham Maslow had presented a theory, which has come to be known as Maslow's Hierarchy of Needs, in the form of a pyramid. He said that physiological (or physical) needs were the most basic and placed them at the base of the pyramid. These were needs that included food, clothing, water, sleep, etc. Then came the safety needs. Once the physical needs were taken care of, an individual seeks safety and security for himself and his loved ones. This involves physical (including health) as well as financial security.

The third level on the list is the need for love and belonging. Once an individual is safe on the physical and safety fronts, he seeks to develop relationships with others. The fourth is the need for esteem—to be valued and validated by others. At the top of the pyramid is the need for self-actualization, after the three other needs are fulfilled. The need for self-actualization thus heralds a stage of personal growth and inner discovery. Thereafter, a sense of contentment sets in.

While the needs of people wary at different levels, what is common is that all of them have the need for the basics to be met, and that includes clean air, clean water, adequate clothing, and basic health and educational facilities.

Figure 1: Maslow's Hierarchy of Needs

But what has Maslow's pyramid got to do with elections in India? How does his theorizing, impressive as it is, impact the results?

To get the answers, let's ask ourselves another question: What does the voter demand or expect from the leaders who contest elections? It's much the same logic that constitutes Maslow's pyramid: food, clothing, water, road, electricity, health and well-being, robust law and order, employment and financial security, a sense of oneness and belonging, respect and admiration, and finally, an environment to achieve a higher level of contentment.

Understanding voter needs can be complicated, but it gets even more complex given the scale and diversity that a country like India offers. Not many realize that India has 600,000 villages and around 6,000 major cities and towns. This rural–urban diversity becomes even more baffling to comprehend when you consider the fact that nearly 70 per cent of the country's population continues to live in villages, and an equivalent proportion of the population depends on agriculture as its primary means of livelihood. This isn't limited to farmers but also those who, indirectly, depend on agricultural activities to sustain themselves—from sellers of fertilizers and farm equipment to those engaged in animal husbandry, fisheries and so on. As a result, the needs of an overwhelming majority of the country revolve around rural and agricultural factors.

India's voting percentages also display a similar rural–urban divide: Of the total 543 Lok Sabha seats that see a direct election, 343 seats comprise purely rural areas, while the remaining 200 seats are a mix of rural–urban and urban areas.[3]

India's rural belt is where the majority of votes come from, and good politicians factor in this reality. The BJP, in 2004, suffered a shock defeat after going into polls with the 'India Shining' campaign: a campaign that was widely perceived as primarily appeasing the urban and the affluent, while neglecting the distress the country's rural areas faced.

But after coming to power in 2014, the party has corrected this. The Modi government had, in its first tenure, except in the first year, constantly increased its agricultural budget. It launched the Pradhan Mantri Kisan Samman Nidhi, which offers direct benefit transfers of ₹6,000 annually to small and marginal farmers with less than two hectares of land. In its election manifesto, the BJP promised to expand the scheme

---

[3]Bansal, Samarth, 'How India Voted in 2019 Election? Here Is What India Today-Axis My India Post-Poll Study Tells Us', *India Today*, 4 June 2019, https://bit.ly/3XZFLV5. Accessed on 2 February 2023.

to other farmers as well.[4] After coming back to power, the Modi government, in its first Cabinet meeting, expanded this scheme to all farmers.[5]

All this has had a direct bearing on its electoral performance. In the 2019 polls, it increased its rural vote share by 6.8 per cent and came back with an even bigger majority, winning 303 seats.[6] Of the 342 rural seats, the BJP won 198, while the Congress, which had traditionally been the stronger party in rural regions, won only 30.[7] As a result, factoring needs becomes crucial for both politicians and the government if they want to perform well and sustain victories.

The needs listed in Maslow's pyramid fall broadly into four categories: social, economic, cultural and aspirational. Social needs are generally demography-specific, relating to gender, age and income. The social needs of a male and a female would evolve in different ways with the passage of time but are initially common. For instance, in rural areas, one of the primary needs among voters is that of food security—fulfilled via the Public Distribution System (PDS)—along

---

[4]Murali, Vani Swarupa, and Diego Maiorano, 'The Rural Vote in the 2019 Indian General Elections', *ISAS Brief*, No. 674, 24 June 2019, https://nus.edu/3YcxCMy. Accessed on 2 February 2023.

[5]Press Information Bureau, 'PM-Kisan Scheme Extension to Include All Eligible Farmer Families Irrespective of the Size of Land Holdings', Ministry of Agriculture & Farmers Welfare, Government of India, 31 May 2019, https://bit.ly/3HkWsmI. Accessed on 2 February 2023.

[6]Murali, Vani Swarupa, and Diego Maiorano, 'The Rural Vote in the 2019 Indian General Elections', *ISAS Brief*, No. 674, 24 June 2019, https://nus.edu/3YcxCMy. Accessed on 2 February 2023.

[7]Bansal, Samarth, 'How India Voted in 2019 Election? Here Is What India Today-Axis My India Post-Poll Study Tells Us', *India Today*, 4 June 2019, https://bit.ly/3XZFLV5. Accessed on 2 February 2023.

with shelter. But as voters attain a certain age, the need that requires to be fulfilled by their parents is one of inoculation (or vaccination).

Especially in rural India, one of the ways that parents will evaluate their leaders in power will be on the basis of easy accessibility to government health centres that provide the vaccination free of cost. Often, these needs change rapidly and are shaped by dynamic circumstances. In such times, voters expect the government to respond just as dynamically and meet their needs as well as their desires.

Nothing illustrates this better than the last few years of our lives, spent through the COVID-19 pandemic. Under the lockdown, where livelihoods of hundreds of millions of people were affected, the poorer sections of society needed urgent supplies of basic essentials like food grains to survive. Migrants, stuck in their workplaces due to the lockdown, needed accessible shelter facilities to stay in, because they ran out of money to pay their rent. Then, as the pandemic progressed, people's needs evolved even more—from drugs and fighting the coronavirus to oxygen supply, and later to vaccine shots.

Voter needs, therefore, are constantly evolving, and a political administrator has to be able to spot those changes and respond to them. For a country with such a massive rural and agrarian population, the needs of most people centre on agrarian issues. Agriculture, for instance, is the top economic issue for most of the country's population.

These economic needs, in turn, fuel social needs. For instance, for farmers and those associated with agriculture to do well, they seek their social and infrastructural needs to be fulfilled—they will want good roads to transport their produce in time; they will need robust storage facilities and warehouses; they will need adequate shops and facilities to meet their needs for fertilizers and other components, as well as repair facilities for their tractors and other farming equipment.

Even the need for an uninterrupted power supply for the rural population is shaped by agriculture. They don't need it to use fancy gadgets and home appliances but primarily for agrarian purposes, from running the water pump that irrigates the fields to operating other farm equipment.

However, a crucial factor that inhibits such an understanding of the country's rural dynamics is the lack of focus that it fetches in the country's media. One very rarely sees media organizations featuring in-depth journalistic pieces that bring to light the day-to-day lives and the trials and tribulations of rural India. The diversity that the country contains is barely reflected in the media's programming, which is mostly concentrated on the lives of urban Indians living in metropolitan cities. This is why, for politicians and governments, a reliance on the media to gain an understanding of rural dynamics can be tricky and deceiving. Media depictions might not be able to reveal fully the complexities involved in the lives and livelihoods of rural India.

People can belong to one particular social or economic section—the low-income group (LIG), the middle-income group (MIG) or the high-income group (HIG)—but even within a group, the cultural desires and needs may be different from one person to another. The need for better health facilities, education, roads, power supply and clothing gets a fillip with the fulfilment of economic needs. When a voter moves from LIG to MIG or even HIG, his choices increase, and his needs tend to match the increase in choices. Political parties talk of the mantra of economic empowerment, but not everyone is able to realize that such an empowerment results in enhanced needs and desires among the voters. The parties that do, or work to, tap into it perform better at the hustings.

Thus, the important factor to remember is that voter needs evolve; they don't remain static. A good politician should have the vision to foresee this evolution and provide for it accordingly. In rural areas, for instance, a social need that is more pronounced is the availability of good schools for children. Primary education thus becomes a factor by which political leaders and their parties are evaluated on their performance. If the party in power has been able to provide a network of schools in villages, parents would be positively impacted and that would contribute to their voting choices.

These needs, as mentioned earlier, continue to evolve. Once a child's education is completed, right from school to college, fresh needs arise—those of employment and income generation. Now, the child is no longer a child, but a youth, and they are now able to frame their political choices based on their new needs. By then, both the social and economic needs have come into play. The accomplishment of a particular need can, and often does, lead to a raising of the bar and a slew of fresh and upscale needs.

The other day, I received a call from an acquaintance in Madhya Pradesh. He had received ₹2 lakh from the central government's Pradhan Mantri Awas Yojana, under which the targeted segment was entitled to ₹2.5 lakh to construct their homes. I thought he would be delighted, but he seemed agitated. I soon learnt the reason for his mood. He told me that while he was yet to get the balance of ₹50,000, other individuals who just got added to the scheme had also received their ₹2 lakh. Why, he cried out, was the government adding new beneficiaries when the old ones had still not got their full amount? The fact that he had already received a substantial sum did not seem to satisfy him; his need had risen by some notches.

The scenario is as follows: You don't have the means to afford two square meals a day. The government decides to distribute free food grains. You accept it with gratitude, thanking the government for meeting your need. But with a regular supply of the food grains, your basic requirement for food is now fulfilled. You move towards scrutinizing the quality of the grains, desiring and demanding a better quality. From quality, you start looking for variety and more nutritious food. Your aspirational needs have gone up from free food to free, quality food and from there to free, quality and more varied food.

While the needs of different sections of people are varied and their expectations from the government also vary in accordance with their needs, the one section that has come into prominence is the youth. This is more so in the case of India that has a youthful (in the age group of 18–35) demographic profile. A Government of India report released in 2022 says that 27.2 per cent of the country's population falls between the age group 15–29 years.[8] The report says that the youth population in the country was estimated to have crossed 371.4 million in 2021.

In 2014, when the new government of Prime Minister Narendra Modi came to power, India had 356 million in the age group of 10–24 years, according to a report from the

---

[8]'Youth in India 2022 Report', *JournalsOfIndia*, 15 July 2022, https://bit.ly/3lCXy6g. Accessed on 14 February 2023.

United Nations.[9] By 2021, India was home to one-fifth of the world's youth population, and more than 62 per cent of the country's population was aged between 15 and 59 years.[10] It is a demographic advantage that few other countries can boast about, and it only natural that the needs and aspirations of this section of the population, many of them being voters, have assumed prime importance.

While the younger generation's social, cultural and economic needs are taken care of by their parents in the early stages, once they are financially independent, they evolve their own unique needs—which they expect their political leaders to fulfil.

The new generation does not choose its friends on considerations of caste, religion or income. As voters, therefore, they have to be dealt with differently from the earlier generation of voters. Besides, they are independent-minded when it comes to making political choices because, unlike their parents and their preceding generations, they do not carry the burden of past allegiances rooted in caste, religion or even ideology.

In our experience in the field, we have seen how the youth prioritize jobs and economic development, as well as things to allow them to realize their aspirations for a better lifestyle and a prosperous career. Though employment opportunities have increased in India, the scale is not proportionate to the increase in youth population.

---

[9]PTI, 'India Has World's Largest Youth Population: UN Report', *The Economic Times*, 18 November 2014, https://bit.ly/2C7dHGA. Accessed on 3 February 2023.

[10]'One of The Youngest Populations in the World—India's Most Valuable Asset', Economic Diplomacy Division, Ministry of External Affairs, 13 June 2021, https://bit.ly/3jqSMId. Accessed on 3 February 2023.

Across the country, the youth believe that a corruption-free government that can deliver suitable livelihood options for them is what they need to move ahead in their lives.

It's no longer the case that the elder of the family decides on the voting preference, to which the others in the family dutifully adhere. Unlike the past where the elder's voice was supreme, today's youth do not necessarily listen to their father let alone heed political leaders blindly. With the power of technology, the youth can better evaluate leaders and thus make the choices that they feel are right for them.

Not only do the youth, with a greater level of awareness, vote according to their own assessment, they also educate and inform the elders in the family on the strengths and weaknesses of leaders and political parties. This is a new but expanding phenomenon across the country.

Apart from demography, a major factor that shapes the country's politics and the way voters respond to politics and politicians is caste. Since the ancient Vedic times, the country's *varna* (a classification primarily based on occupation) system has been the foundation of stratifying and categorizing society as per their livelihoods and roles in society. The four varnas—Brahmin, Kshatriya, Vaishya and Shudra—were based on a social hierarchy that was dependent upon their roles and livelihoods in society. The Brahmins were the priestly class, the teachers and intellectuals primarily tasked with the knowledge of religion and the Vedas. The Kshatriyas were the warrior class, whose task was mainly to fight, bring stability and govern. The Vaishyas were the merchants, who were primarily involved in commerce, from trading to running businesses, handling finances and even agriculture. The Shudras were mainly where society derived its labour from—the workers and artisans came from this class.

The varnas were a way of bringing social order and ensuring a streamlined system of employment in society. Dalits and tribals were left out of this system and were called *avarna* (being without any varna). Many have argued that the varna system was flexible, in which people could change their varnas based on their skill sets and proficiencies. However, over time, the varnas solidified and led to the more rigid caste system coming into place. Many have argued that the varna system solidified into castes as an advent of the modern colonial rule, where the British, in an attempt to classify society into categories they could easily understand, hardened the caste lines.

Caste has become an important and integral part of social identity in India and, as a result, has also become an influential factor shaping the country's politics. There are multiple ways in which caste has come to play a crucial factor. One is through such caste groups coming to influence political parties, either becoming their backers or not, depending on the party's inclinations.

For instance, the BJP has traditionally been seen as a party that is of and for upper-caste groups. It has constantly been backed by these groups and has, in turn, been seen as an active backer of these caste groups. In the 2022 Uttar Pradesh state elections, for instance, voting data showed that the overwhelming majority of upper-caste groups, like the Brahmins, Rajputs and Baniyas voted for the BJP—as much as 89 per cent in some cases. Colloquially, the BJP has often been known as the 'Brahmin–Baniya' party. But this reputation has been overturned, in some ways, with the advent of Modi in the prime minister's chair. Belonging to an Other Backward Class (OBC) group himself (Ghanchi-Teli), Modi has managed to reorient the party's focus to a much broader social coalition; as a result, its support base is now much more diverse, gaining support from diverse caste groups.

There are also parties that are focussed on specific caste groups and derive their identity, mostly, from those caste groups. For instance, the Samajwadi Party (SP) has extensively focussed on its Yadav base and derived its identity from that base. Similarly, the Rashtriya Lok Dal has maintained a special focus on the Jats and gains its politico-social capital from the community.

The role of castes in politics has also evolved with time. For instance, traditionally, while the Congress relied on an umbrella coalition of castes driven by upper caste support, this started to change. By the 1960s, the anti-Brahmin movement came to power in Tamil Nadu with the political party Dravida Munnetra Kazhagam (DMK) making anti-Brahminism its political calling card. In the north, the emergence of caste leaders from backward groups, like Karpoori Thakur and Charan Singh, also started to drive a wedge into the Congress's support base.

In August 1990, V.P. Singh, the then prime minister, announced his government's decision to accept the recommendations of the Mandal Commission and extend 27 per cent reservation to members of the OBC groups. The reservation heralded a new era of caste identity-driven politics in the country and gave way to the emergence of new leaders who would aggressively court caste groups as their primary voter base. Two of the most significant parties that capitalized on this caste assertion were Mulayam Singh Yadav's SP and Lalu Prasad Yadav's Rashtriya Janata Dal (RJD).

As backward groups slowly started consolidating with

leaders and parties that openly identified with their backward caste identities, a similar situation unfolded among the Dalit community. Among the Dalits, leaders like Jagjivan Ram and Kanshi Ram, among others, started increasing the political visibility of Dalits in the country's politics. Even within Dalits, there was a schism with the Bahujan Samaj Party (BSP) appealing more to the Jatav Dalits, leaving the non-Jatavs open to be wooed by other parties like the Congress in the past and the BJP now.

Among the tribal communities, there have been attempts to organize them through political parties like the Jharkhand Mukti Morcha, which seeks to draw its base from Jharkhand's tribal population, as well as smaller, regional parties like the Bharatiya Tribal Party in Gujarat and the Tripura-based TIPRA, which is the Tipraha Indigenous Progressive Regional Alliance of the royal scion, Pradyot Kishore Debbarman.

But the biggest proof of the fact that the country's tribal population hasn't aligned itself with any one party lies in a small, nondescript Lok Sabha constituency on the tip of Gujarat, the seat of Valsad, reserved for members of the Scheduled Tribe (ST) constituencies. The ST reserved seat has constantly switched loyalties with nearly each passing Lok Sabha poll, and has, in fact, become a bellwether seat for the country's politics. For over five decades now, the seat has consistently and unfailingly elected candidates from parties that have gone on to form a government in New Delhi. Be it in 1977 when the Janata Party swept the Congress away in the post-Emergency fury, or in 1980 when the Congress roared back to power, or in 1989 when the V.P. Singh-led Janata Dal (JD) formed the government, this seat has consistently flipped sides and elected candidates from parties that have gone on to become the ruling party at the Centre. For pollsters like me, this constituency has become the seat to watch out for in every Lok Sabha poll!

Similarly, religious identity has also shaped the country's politics, with voters of different religious groups being lured by various political parties to become the foundation for those parties. Traditionally, the Congress has courted the Muslim community as one of its steadfast vote bases. But this has been challenged in many states, like in Uttar Pradesh by the SP and in Bihar by the RJD. Similarly, the Hindu community, from ardently backing the Congress post Independence, has been aggressively wooed by the BJP now.

The needs of all these religious groups and castes evolve and the challenge for parties and leaders has been to keep up with these evolving needs. When groups see that parties are no longer able to match up, they switch sides and hedge their bets on who they believe will be best suited to deliver.

All needs do not have the same scale of impact. High prices, poor roads, irregular electricity, lack of potable water, etc. have a universal connect. If these needs are not fulfilled, no matter the place, voters are unlikely to ignore such a failure on the part of their rulers. But there are other needs that are not as universal. For instance, in states with a robust agrarian base, an issue like unemployment might not strike a chord with too many voters. Similarly, in some states where the policing is fairly competent, the issue of law and order doesn't become a major electoral point. But in others, where poor law and order is a major factor, the issue becomes an electoral one.

We are all familiar with the terms, 'pro-incumbency' and 'anti-incumbency'. The accepted wisdom is that pro-incumbency is associated with the good work done by an incumbent regime while anti-incumbency is a reflection of its failures. But pro-incumbency can also relate to the people's perception of who they think is best suited to tackle the challenges they face—who is better equipped to actualize the needs of the voters, in other words.

In summary, individual and community needs, therefore, drive the choices that people, or voters, make.

But it's not just the voters that are driven by needs. The second pivot of electoral politics, the leader, is also affected by these needs. But as we shall see, the leader's needs are determined by an entirely different set of factors, and those factors eventually result in the choices they make.

2

NEEDS AND THE LEADER

India, after Independence, has seen no dearth of powerful political leaders emerging at both the national as well as the regional level. One of the categories through which independent India's leaders can be filtered is whether they belong to families of political leaders or not, i.e., if they are political dynasts or not. This has been an important classification even in colonial India, when political dynasties like the Nehrus, the Abdullahs in Jammu and Kashmir, the Shuklas in Madhya Pradesh, etc. were strong.

But what makes this distinction between dynasts and non-dynasts so important to address is the growing traction it has had in Indian contemporary politics since the last decade or so. The BJP has repeatedly trained its guns on dynastic opposition parties and decried such familial political inheritance. But even the BJP has not been able to evade a dynastic trend—from Rajnath Singh to its own Gandhis (mother–son duo of Maneka and Varun) to Anurag Thakur. Some of its top leaders are either products of dynastic politics or its perpetrators.[11] At least 11 per cent of its Members of Parliament (MPs) now belong to political families.[12]

Beyond the political discourse surrounding it, the background of the leaders is a vital factor that shapes their relationship with their electorate as well as the bureaucracy. The leaders' background, especially whether they belong to political dynasties or not, determines what their needs are, how they prioritize these needs and the choices they make to meet these needs.

Dynasts are those who owe their position and privilege to their family name and legacy. The names that readily come to mind are Indira Gandhi, Rahul Gandhi, M.K. Stalin, Pankaja Munde, H.D. Kumaraswamy, Jyotiraditya Scindia, Akhilesh Yadav, Sachin Pilot, Naveen Patnaik and many more. On the other hand, the non-dynast leaders are those that have made it big in politics without the advantage of a family legacy. They may have risen from the political ranks over decades, such as Morarji Desai, Atal Bihari Vajpayee, Manmohan Singh, P.V. Narasimha Rao, Lalu Prasad Yadav, H.D. Deve Gowda, Chandra Shekhar, Sharad Yadav, Mamata Banerjee and Narendra Modi, among others. Or, they may have been products of movements and causes, like George Fernandes, Arvind Kejriwal and L.K. Advani. Kejriwal emerged out of the anti-corruption movement launched by the social activist Anna Hazare, while Advani shot into the limelight with the

[11]Pandey, Neelam, 'Bjp Says It Doesn't Believe in Dynastic Politics, but Its List of Dynast Leaders Is Ever-Growing', *The Print*, 2 August 2021, https://bit.ly/3X10LJG. Accessed on 6 February 2023.

[12]Arnimesh, Shanker, and Neelam Pandey, 'BJP's List of Dynasts Is Only Growing Longer, It Now Includes at Least 11% of Its MPs', *The Print*, 22 July 2020, https://bit.ly/40v8L8N. Accessed on 6 February 2023.

Ayodhya Ram Temple campaign and Fernandes became known through his trade union activism.

Of course, there are also those who were neither dynasts nor did they come out of any particularly identifiable mass movement, although they had a privileged background—that of a feudal environment, for instance. V.P. Singh is a good example, and so are Digvijaya Singh and Captain Amarinder Singh, although it must be added that V.P. Singh became a leader in his own right after he led the anti-corruption drive within his own Congress party, quit the organization and implemented the Mandal Commission's recommendations on providing reservations to the OBCs.

The origins of leaders determine their needs and the priorities they accord to those needs. The need that is uppermost in the mind of a dynast is the benefit for his family. A dynast occupies a high position in the political space primarily because of his family legacy, and it is to the family name that he owes his status. It is natural, therefore, for him to accord primacy to family concerns. A leader who is a product of dynasty does not have to be beholden to the people for the position he occupies. For him, family comes first, then the party, and thereafter the people and governance. Often, dynasts can be disconnected from ordinary people's lives because of their privileged upbringing. This is detrimental because such dynasts, often, can't understand or relate to the grievances of their voters and have little sense of the struggles they face.

For instance, when we tried to do a post-poll survey to find out the reasons behind the shocking defeat of a leader who is a second-generation dynast, on a seat which had been represented by his family for decades now, voters echoed the sentiment of the politician being disconnected with the grievances of the people. Multiple voters told us how they rejected the dynast because he would barely visit the constituency. Instead, he had made homes in Delhi and in the state capital. One voter told us that every time someone wanted an audience with this dynast, they would have to trudge all the way to Delhi or the state capital to meet him. When he wasn't even around to see their pain, how would he understand and alleviate them, is a question on most of the voters' minds. Not surprisingly, he suffered a humiliating defeat in the 2019 polls. Of course, there have been leaders with a family legacy who, later on, did maintain considerable contact with the people, but that was after the family name secured them their position.

On the other hand, the priorities of non-dynast leaders are starkly different. Since the non-dynast has emerged out of a cause or a movement, or risen to the top from humble origins, he relates completely with the people and their problems. His main priority is, therefore, the masses, because it is to the people and not to his family that he owes his political position, and it is on their indulgence that he banks his sustainability. Once the people accord him acceptability, the party is compelled to give him a prominent role to play. His acceptability thus grows from the bottom-up. Leaders such as Modi and Sharad Pawar are good examples. For them, people come first and family is the last priority. This is not to say that they do not promote their family—some, like Sharad Pawar, have done it—but by and large, their politics is people-centric.

This contrast is seen even in the schemes and welfare benefits that non-dynasts conceive and execute as their flagship schemes. For instance, a non-dynast leader like Nitish Kumar could conceive of a scheme to give bicycles to girl students as a way to encourage their mobility and education. Similarly, another non-dynast leader like Shivraj Singh Chouhan conceived the flagship scheme, the Ladli Laxmi Yojna, which allots scholarships to girl students incrementally as they continue their studies. It can get very difficult for dynasts to conceive and believe in such schemes because they can be disconnected from the everyday struggles of the poorer, vulnerable sections of the population.

However, Odisha's chief minister, Naveen Patnaik, is an exception to this. Bureaucrats who have been close to the chief minister have told me how Patnaik has been clear about his priority ever since he assumed power: strengthening and making the state's food grain delivery through PDS as efficient as possible. These bureaucrats talked about the core of Patnaik's administration—that when a leader steps in and fulfils the role that the family's breadwinner is traditionally supposed to, the leader's place gets cemented unshakeably within the family. This belief is reflected in the thinking of Modi's administration too—from its focus on ensuring the swift delivery of services like gas cylinders to homes for the poor to transferring money directly into bank accounts.

In our interactions with voters, especially in rural seats where dynasts have been elected repeatedly, people often told me how they find it so difficult to connect with these dynast leaders and convey their problems to them. Dynasts rarely live among them but are rather mostly located in bigger cities nearby, and even when they visit, they come in chopper sorties or chartered aircrafts. Voters hardly feel any sense of being relatable with such leaders, especially when they are struggling to eke out a living.

The ecosystem of the non-dynast, unlike a dynast who has a family legacy to maintain, revolves around acceptability among the people. On the other hand, the dynast is acceptable to the public because of his family name and hence, his priority often revolves around safeguarding the family's reputation. This, the dynast often feels, is the key to his sustained public popularity. Hence, his decisions would be influenced by, above all, family considerations.

Oftentimes, my interactions with political dynasts show that they can be complacent about their voter needs while in powers because they know that their identity as political dynasts, will exist and sustain them even if they cannot perform. One dynast I interacted with, after coming to power, showed no urgency in delivering on the promises that he had campaigned for. Instead, he said he could wait for a few more years before he started delivering them! As against this, non-dynasts are faced with a sense of urgency in their performance because they can be easily replaced if they do not perform to expectations.

It is possible that the voters give a longer rope to the dynasts and are willing to wait longer for delivery. While this may have been the case in the earlier decades when the superior–subordinate connect worked with the masses, it is no longer valid today, with the baggage of family legacy having little to no impression over the voters.

It would be apt to take the example of the Congress party. Even at the state level, several leaders have come to the forefront because of their family connections. This is because the dynast phenomenon drives the party from the top, thus creating an ecosystem that affords primacy to family-driven leaders at all levels. Indira Gandhi depended on Sanjay Gandhi and, later, on Rajiv Gandhi, even though there were several prominent and capable leaders in the party to whom she could have passed the baton.

When Sonia Gandhi came into politics, she was not a dynast in the traditional sense. Her upbringing was abroad and in a non-political family. Even after her marriage into a political family in India, she remained away from politics, to begin with. She passed on a chance to become the country's prime minister and instead chose Manmohan Singh for the high post. Singh had impeccable credentials as an economist of global repute and a slew of achievements as the country's finance minister during Narasimha Rao's term as prime minister when he executed massive economic reforms, including the abolishing of the licence-permit-quota raj.

However, the urge to keep the family uppermost in the mind was never far from Sonia Gandhi's mind, even as she adapted to the ecosystem that she inherited through marriage. The emergence of the so-called 'Rahul brigade', a term often used in the media to describe Rahul Gandhi's acolytes, mostly drawn from political families and promoted rapidly in the Congress ranks, is one such example of the ecosystem. Many, from this group of young leaders of roughly the same age as Rahul, had a family legacy to maintain, like him. Many of the group's members became MPs, Members of the Legislative Assembly (MLAs) and ministers. Often, Prime Minister Singh used to be criticized for the influence that the Gandhis were said to have been exerting on his administration. One recalls the infamous case when Rahul Gandhi tore up an ordinance cleared by the Manmohan Singh Cabinet before the media.

While it becomes natural for a dynast to first take care of family needs while the other needs are listed way below in the order of priority, for the non-dynast, family considerations have to be kept at a distance. It has been reported that after Deve Gowda became the prime minister, he asked his top bureaucrats to not succumb to pressures that his family members, his sons especially, might bring upon them and the bureaucratic system. He supposedly remarked that at times, he might publicly concur with their needs out of consideration for his family, but the administration must do only that which is correct.

For the dynast, family is his political equity; for the non-dynast, his political equity is the connection he has with the masses. Often, a non-dynast leader is better-placed than a dynast to conceive and execute strategies that are unique and display a better relationship with the masses.

In 1974, Sharad Yadav was a young socialist leader with no base to speak of. He was handpicked by Jayaprakash Narayan as the unified opposition candidate to take on the Goliath, the Congress party, at the peak of its political strength. Yadav, who rose from the grassroots as a student leader, was no match for the Congress party's resources and its organizational strength. So, he had to do something different if he wanted to stand a chance. Yadav tapped into the army of cycle-rickshaw drivers that the city had—a trick that worked on different levels. Suddenly, he had organizational manpower to campaign for him, but that stunt also helped to endear himself to voters who saw his humble origins and backed him. Yadav won the by-poll, and that victory is seen as the beginning of the decline of the Congress. Decades later, Kejriwal too depended on similar foot soldiers to take his political campaign forward in the Delhi Legislative Assembly elections—the autorickshaw drivers, for instance.

The primacy of needs of a mass-based leader also depends on his following. Someone like Lalu Prasad Yadav or Mulayam Singh Yadav cultivated their Yadav caste vote bank, and together with the backing of the Muslim voters, carved a successful political career for themselves despite not generally winning over the other sections of society. Mayawati too depended largely on the Dalit vote bank to catapult her to a pole position in the politics of Uttar Pradesh. Of course, given that she owed her position also to Kanshi Ram, she never forgets to pay respects to him. In several government advertisements that were released when she was chief minister, the mention of Kanshi Ram was in abundance. It is obvious that, once in power, the first need of these leaders is to appease their respective vote banks.

Among the non-dynasts, there are leaders who have been selected to high positions of power, and such leaders have their own needs. I.K. Gujral and Manmohan Singh are two good examples. The first became prime minister of a non-Congress government that was entirely dependent on the Congress for continuance in office. The second became prime minister because he was chosen by a party president who was far more politically powerful than he was. The primary need of the two leaders thus revolved around keeping the leaders, whom they owed their chair to, in good humour. When Gujral lost the Congress chief's confidence, he had to quit. In Manmohan Singh's case, we are aware of the many reports that spoke of his subordination to the wishes of the Congress president who had given him the post. Because such leaders have no mass base, nor do they have a family legacy, they are dependent on another powerful leader, and the needs of that leader become their needs too.

The reason why a leader's origins matter a lot is because it is now fairly clear that their origins shape their style of governance. One way of seeing this is how political leaders interact with the bureaucracy.

There is, often, a very distinct way in which dynast and non-dynast leaders handle the bureaucracy. A dynast, for instance, keeping his family legacy in mind, shies away from taking bold decisions and, instead, asks the bureaucracy to implement them. He is fearful that the decisions could result in controversies and sully the family's name, and he has no idea of how even people-friendly decisions can be implemented without getting into trouble. Besides, he has little understanding of the grievances at the grassroots level. He is cautious to a fault.

Such a contrast can be seen best in Uttar Pradesh, with the two successive governments of Akhilesh Yadav, followed by Yogi Adityanath. Both of them were first-timers in the chief minister's chair, but Yadav dithered on taking big decisions or cracking the whip on errant leaders of his own party. In stark contrast, Adityanath realized that he would have to take bold decisions in order to establish his own identity as a tough taskmaster, even if it meant angering his own party's leaders. The first was a dynast and the other, a non-dynast, and that reflected in their way of functioning.

The non-dynast, too, may have little understanding of the babu culture, but he has the power, derived directly from the people, to insist on measures that the bureaucracy has to implement. His mandate is to maintain his popularity and popular support. His direction is, simply put, somewhat like this: 'Do it. How it is to be done, is your problem!' Several populist measures get implemented in such a fashion.

Clever leaders like Modi lean on the bureaucracy but have also, over time, learned its nitty-gritty to ensure that they do not fall into traps later on and that the bureaucracy does not engage in questionable ways to implement their decisions. On the other hand, less informed leaders such as Lalu Prasad Yadav or Om Prakash Chautala landed in trouble because they neither had knowledge of the bureaucracy's functioning nor did they care to make sure that wrong methods were not used to implement their orders. They were content so long as they gained from those decisions.

But normally, leaders who come from the grassroots are less prone to be taken for a ride by the babus and are quicker in learning the ropes. Mayawati learnt the tricks of using the bureaucracy, as did many other grassroots leaders. Such leaders are blunt, straightforward and confident. They have the support of the people and can, without the risk of a political fallout, take on the babus if they desire to do so. As a result, the delivery of welfare schemes and programmes are faster with a non-dynast at the helm.

Even Prime Minister Narendra Modi, before he took up the high post, had mentioned his working style to be somewhat similar. He had said that he doesn't read long files prepared by his bureaucracy. Instead, he tells his team of bureaucrats to read and absorb them, summarize them and give him an oral briefing. Modi, then, takes a decision based on that briefing and his contextual understanding of the subject.[13]

However, an understanding of the bureaucracy is not enough. If a leader himself possesses knowledge in a domain of his expertise, it helps him to make informed choices that the bureaucracy has to execute. Union Cabinet Minister Nitin

---

[13]Patel, Aakar, 'Note Ban Success: Test of PM's Working Style', *Deccan Chronicle*, 11 December 2016, https://bit.ly/3I05mHJ. Accessed on 6 February 2023.

Gadkari is a case in point. He is neither a dynast nor does he have a family legacy, but he has been an astute businessman. Thus, he understands issues from the perspective of both a lawmaker and a businessman and appreciates the need for the two to work in tandem for the greater public good. He is known for quick and clarity-driven decision-making, and his ministry is known to implement projects in a time-bound manner with minimum cost overruns, if any. It's an issue of man-management. While he trusts the bureaucrats and gives them the support and freedom to operate, he does not allow them to dictate terms or mislead him.

A contrary case in point is Rajiv Gandhi. He was well-intentioned, sincere and determined to make a positive difference. But he had no hold over the bureaucracy and his assorted advisors. The result was that he landed in trouble over various issues, including that of the Bofors scam. His bureaucrats made a mess of the controversy, and he ended up having egg on his face. Some of his decisions turned controversial—the Shah Bano case, for example—where he was influenced by the coterie around him.

There is an interesting side to the dynast's dependence on his family. In a majority of the cases, it is the son that has caused embarrassment and political trouble. This might be speculative, but often, driving his attitude towards work is the fact that he has got their political support on a platter, thanks to the family name. Proving himself through his work is not something he has needed to rely on.

Such reliance on the family name often leads to a misuse of power that the parents, also political leaders, wield. Take Indira Gandhi's son Sanjay Gandhi, Morarji Desai's son or Sonia Gandhi's son, for example. Daughters, on the other hand, have been less of a problem. From Indira Gandhi to the Nationalist Congress Party (NCP) supremo Sharad Pawar's daughter Supriya Sule, or even Sushmita Dev, the daughter of the Congress veteran Santosh Mohan Dev, these daughters have been political assets to their parents.

But whoever the leader may be, dynast or not, he owes a certain amount of responsibility towards his parents and offspring. This is more so in India. In the West, often, by the time children reach the age of 17 or so, they are told to be financially independent. They take loans for higher studies and then pay back through their own earnings. It is different in India. Handholding is done by the parents of their children, and then by the children of their parents. So, even if a leader is a non-dynast, his family does expect some political consideration from the leader. The needs of leaders, dynasts or not, are thus impacted by family considerations, more in the first case and far less in the second.

With power come many bad habits and bad needs. The leader has to oblige his family, his party and his constituents, among others. There is sacrifice and compromise. The bigger the ecosystem, the greater are the challenges. If a leader's personal and professional record is clean, he can counter such challenges more effectively. Wrong decisions are seen by the public as genuine mistakes and not driven by ulterior motives. But if there are chinks in the armour by way of bad needs and habits, then those challenges can take a leader down the drain.

We have seen various examples of power being misused by family members in the recent past—Ajay Mishra Teni's son Ashish Mishra, who is accused of running over farmers in Lakhimpur Kheri, Uttar Pradesh, during a protest march against the controversial farm laws[14]; Akash Vijayvargiya, a BJP MLA and son of senior BJP leader Kailash Vijayvargiya, who was caught on camera thrashing a municipal corporation officer with a cricket bat in Indore (the officers were in the area for an anti-encroachment drive)[15]; P. Chidambaram's son Karti Chidambaram, who is facing alleged corruption and money laundering charges[16]; former Maharashtra Chief Minister Vilasrao Deshmukh, who visited the battered Taj Mahal Palace hotel in Mumbai with his actor–son Riteish and filmmaker Ram Gopal Varma, triggering angry reactions from Mumbaikars[17]; not to forget high-profile leaders like Sanjay Gandhi's, M.K. Stalin's and Lalu Prasad Yadav's sons and kins who have been surrounded by several controversies in the past.

One finds at the famous Konark Temple the Gajasimha sculpture, which features a lion right on top, an elephant right below and a man at the lowest level. The lion is a symbol of pride and power, associated with Goddess Durga, and the elephant is a symbol of wealth, associated with Goddess Laxmi. The sculpture tells a profound story. When man is burdened with pride, wealth and power and does not know ways to

---

[14]Pandey, Alok, 'Union Minister's Son, Accused of Running Over Farmers in Up, Gets Bail', *NDTV*, 10 February 2022, https://bit.ly/3DIVTlQ. Accessed on 6 February 2023.

[15]Times Now, 'On Cam: Kailash Vijayvargiya's MLA Son Assaults Govt Official with Cricket Bat, Booked', *The Economic Times*, 26 June 2019, https://bit.ly/3HFd8Fs. Accessed on 6 February 2023.

[16]Express News Service, 'After CBI, ED Books Karti Chidambaram on Charges of Money Laundering in Chinese Visas Case', *The Indian Express*, 26 May 2022, https://bit.ly/3RxHFtz. Accessed on 6 February 2023.

[17]India News, 'Deshmukh Visit to Taj with Ram Gopal Varma Sparks Anger', *Hindustan Times*, 1 December 2008, https://bit.ly/3DEc6IT. Accessed on 6 February 2023.

handle them, he is bound to be eventually crushed. This is true of our leaders when they prioritize their needs on narrow considerations.

~

3

BUREAUCRACY: THE INVISIBLE THREAD

An often-invisible thread links the fortunes of leaders to their voters—the bureaucracy.

Sardar Vallabhbhai Patel, independent India's first deputy prime minister, had once called the Indian Civil Services the 'steel frame of India' that was critical in ensuring good governance. But ever since its inception, this steel frame has shown remarkable elasticity in adapting to the needs and aspirations of the political class while also keeping in mind that it had to largely follow the established rules and regulations. The needs and choices of the bureaucracy are determined by the directives the ruling political ecosystem issues. But in spite of that, the bureaucracy remains a vital component in the performance of governments and leaders.

Regardless of what the political parties or leaders think or say, nothing happens without the execution on the ground. The executing arm is the vast and mind-boggling network of bureaucrats who manage the system—from the Gram Panchayat level, all the way up to the highest levels of national administration. The bridge between the leader and the people, when it comes to execution and performance, is the bureaucracy. But because the buck ultimately stops at the desk of the political ruler, he has to make sure that the bureaucracy gets him the results he desires. Thus, in a way, the leader's fortunes are tied intricately with that of the bureaucracy.

Yet, the relationship between a leader and the bureaucracy seldom features in discourses around politics and governance. It is the ecosystem of bureaucrats and officials that translates leaders' vision to action. The real test of the mettle of leaders lies in how effectively they manage to get the bureaucracy to work towards their vision and goals.

But this powerful bureaucracy is plagued with various ailments. Prime Minister Rajiv Gandhi had famously remarked that, out of a rupee allotted by the government for the poor and the needy through various welfare programmes, only 15 paise reached the intended beneficiary. The unsaid part was that the rest of the 85 paise got stuck in the bureaucratic maze, and various arms of officialdom ensured that the money never reached the target beneficiary.

More recently, Union Minister Nitin Gadkari has repeatedly and publicly berated the bureaucracy and blamed its officials for the languid pace of progress on crucial infrastructure projects.The execution of nearly every amenity, including essential services such as roads, health and education, is managed by the bureaucrats. The execution involves not just the fructification of the service but three other important components: quality, quantity and time-bound delivery. All three elements are critical, and, often indispensable. For any service to be effective, it has to have the right proportion of these components.

Let's take the example of education. The preferred choice of school for a parent for his ward is the private sector. This is because government primary schools often carry a bad reputation (with a few exceptions) for the poor quality of teaching they impart. The quality of education is critical because it serves as the foundation of the child's life—the foundation of his training, skill and beliefs. If the foundation is weak, nothing can sustain him later. Can a tree, sowed in a small pot, ever blossom and offer fruit the way a tree growing in the wild does? Unlikely. For the same reason, parents are unwilling to take chances and do whatever it takes to send their children for private schooling, even though they have to spend more by way of fees and other education-related costs.

On the other hand, when it comes to higher education, the first choice is government-managed institutions, whether it be in the field of medicine, engineering, management or even law. The quality of learning in government-managed higher institutions is better and the fee structure is reasonable. Private institutions charge exorbitant fees and the quality they provide is often not commensurate with the money they charge. In many cases, private institutions have become money-raking enterprises with little regard for the quality of education they provide.

Thus, for primary education, people avoid government schools, whereas for higher education, they throng to government colleges. However, the quantity of such good-quality government institutions is inadequate, thereby creating intense competition for the limited seats up for grabs. Inadequate seats lead to a problem of inaccessibility for vast sections of the population, leaving them discontent with and disgruntled at the government. Hence, not just quality, but quantity matters in governance.

Similarly, both quality and quantity are also important in services such as health and roads. In many remote areas of the country, there are not enough primary or tertiary healthcare centres. According to the World Bank's latest available data till 2017, India has only 0.5 beds per 1,000 people, whereas the global average is nearly six times higher—at 2.9 beds per 1,000 people.[18]

Nothing illustrates this better than the state of our healthcare, even in our capital. In July 2022, a woman delivered her baby outside the well-known Safdarjung Hospital, just metres away from a dustbin, nearly 15 hours after she had reached the hospital to get herself admitted. Her family members told the media that the hospital authorities had delayed the admission despite their repeated pleas to get her admitted.[19]

Even though in the past few years, the numbers of government-managed hospitals, both in the primary and tertiary sectors, have increased substantially, they are still not enough, and the quality remains a matter of concern in many cases. The same is true of roads. Important cities and highways have good quality roads, but the interior locations still have to make do with poorly constructed roads that cave in often, at times under the smallest rainfall.

The food grains supplied through the PDS is another example. In many cases, the quality of the supply is poor—

---

[18]'Hospital Beds (per 1,000 People)—India, World', *The World Bank*, https://bit.ly/3wZRUgU. Accessed on 6 February 2023.

[19]'Viral: Woman Delivers Baby Near Dustbin outside Safdarjung Hospital after Waiting for Hours', *The Times of India*, 20 July 2022, https://bit.ly/3KzcsVe. Accessed on 24 February 2023.

certainly poorer than what is available in the open market. The beneficiary, on paper, thus gets the benefit of low-cost or even free food grains, but he is compelled to consume poor quality food. There have been many instances of the beneficiaries selling their PDS quota of rations and using the money to buy better quality food grains in the open market. Efforts have been made to address the problem, but again, a lot more needs to be done.

Time-bound delivery is arguably the most important of the three components. Even if the quantity and quality issues are satisfactorily addressed, little is achieved—either in political terms or bureaucratic accomplishment—if the benefits do not reach the targeted audience in time. For instance, there is little purpose in delivering high-quality food grains after a family is struck by starvation. The scheme is meant to prevent precisely such a crisis and, hence, timely delivery is crucial.

Similarly, if crucial medicines or supplies of life-saving equipment are not available during a medical crisis, acquiring it after the crisis is over is redundant. Also, it isn't enough only to ensure the construction of hospitals or just focus on enrolling more doctors. Both have to happen simultaneously. There is little purpose in having hospitals with doctors at a distance that is out of reach for most people; having hospitals without adequate doctors; or having both adequate hospitals and doctors, but not having medicines and equipment in those hospitals.

If roads take more time than is reasonably necessary, it adversely impacts the people who are in dire need of good connectivity. Besides, delays in delivery of goods and services also results in cost overruns, the burden of which is often borne by the ordinary, law-abiding taxpayer.

In all these instances, the role of the bureaucracy is critical if services have to be delivered in superior quality, adequate quantity and within the desired timeframe. If the bureaucratic machinery is on its toes, it can tackle these aspects.

Increasingly, ambitious and sharp politicians in power are realizing just how important an effective bureaucracy can be to the government's performance and, in turn, to their own political fortunes. As a result, top leaders are empowering bureaucrats and, often, reaching out to them, cutting out even their own junior ministers, to ensure timely and efficient performances and deliveries of government schemes. Obviously, ministers are not too happy with this but have little choice if their leader is powerful enough and people are rewarding the government's performance.

The BJP government, ever since its dominance began in 2014, has constantly focussed on, and taken pride in and credit for the effective delivery of its welfare schemes. It has invested a great amount of work in ensuring that government welfare schemes that are announced don't remain on paper—from using the socio-economic caste census data to identify the beneficiaries of its schemes, transferring funds straight to their bank accounts to even 'geo-tagging',[20] a geographical location-identifying exercise meant to digitally identify the creation of assets under programmes like the Mahatma Gandhi National Rural Employment Guarantee Act (MGNREGA).

On the ground, various journalists have pointed out how such an effective delivery of welfare benefits has been

---

[20]Tewari, Ruhi, 'Geo-Tagging—One of the Secrets behind the Success of Modi Govt's Welfare Schemes', *The Print*, 6 August 2019, https://bit.ly/3I0MmJe. Accessed on 6 February 2023.

instrumental in swinging the election results the BJP's way.[21] One research paper by authors Louise Tillin, Rajeshwari Deshpande and K.K. Kailash also confirmed this, and claimed that while welfare delivery was not a decisive factor, it was seen to have influenced voter choices towards the BJP often.[22]

Even at the state level, the Madhya Pradesh government, under Shivraj Singh Chouhan, has been implementing the Teerth Darshan Yojna, a scheme so smoothly executed that it seems effortless, even when it is anything but. The scheme is meant to take the state's elderly population to Hindu pilgrimage sites for free. Chouhan's administration conceived the scheme so well that citizens seldom faced any issue in accessing the scheme. The smooth implementation of this programme involved immense coordination between IAS officials as well as lower bureaucracy cutting across departments, and could not have been implemented without a firm grip on administration.

However, this machinery, as I have mentioned earlier, often takes its cues from the political leadership, with 'follow the leader' being the maxim. The babu at the block level looks for directions from his immediate superior at the district level, and the bureaucracy at the district seeks instructions from its superior and so on. In a parliamentary democracy such as ours, the buck stops with the prime minister. Therefore, it is the leader at the helm who initiates all the actions that percolate from the top, all the way down to the block and the village

---

[21] Anshuman, Kumar, and Vasudha Venugopal, 'UP Elections: Govt Scheme Beneficiaries Once Again Do the Magic for BJP', *The Economic Times*, 11 March 2022, https://bit.ly/3jGb8Vw. Accessed on 6 February 2023.

[22] Tillin, Louise, 'Do Government's Welfare Schemes Influence the Patterns of Voting?' *Hindustan Times*, 6 December 2019, https://bit.ly/3wWRk3c. Accessed on 6 February 2023.

levels through the bureaucratic system. The bureaucracy's response depends on the thought process, the conduct and the performance of political leaders. Taken together, these three constitute the signal for the bureaucrat to either move ahead or maintain a status quoist position.

It is said that people might not do what you say but they are more likely to follow what you do. This is especially true in case of leaders and voters. A leader can make any number of profound statements, but the people will judge him by his actions, not words. Nearly every political leader swears by Mahatma Gandhi's statements on simple living and ensuring that the last man in line gets the benefits he deserves out of government programmes, but how many of those leaders actually act accordingly?

Often, the bureaucrat observes the conduct of the leader and acts accordingly. If he notices that the politician's actions do not match his words, the bureaucratic machinery will also be less than enthusiastic in implementing the desired actionable plans. If a leader is seen to be wanting to promote vested interests, either his own or those of his family, regardless of his pious statements to the contrary, the bureaucracy will take the hint and will either find ways to help the leader make money or look away. Of course, not every bureaucrat will indulge in blatant wrongdoing, but then, they will have to be prepared to bear the consequences through abrupt transfers or adverse comments in their annual confidential reports. We have sometimes seen bureaucrats become whistle-blowers and expose irregularities within the system, only to be punished by the system.

For example, Ashok Khemka, the IAS officer who had famously initiated inquiries into Sonia Gandhi's son-in-law

Robert Vadra's land deals in Haryana and had even cancelled a ₹58-crore land deal between Vadra and DLF,[23] has been transferred more than 54 times in 29 years of his service.[24] Officers like Khemka, sadly, become irritants for political parties, across ideological barriers, because they often shine light on the rot within the system.

The flip side is that, even if a bureaucrat is crooked-minded, he will be forced to tread the right path if the political leader is honest, transparent and straightforward, and has an effective check on the babus.

One of the things that a good, disciplined leader does is to put into place a system, which involves regular monitoring and creating a system of accountability for these bureaucrats. Such systems ensure that bureaucrats are kept on their toes, since the leader constantly keeps an eye on the timelines and the progress of major schemes or projects through such mechanisms. For instance, many leaders are now coming up with 'war rooms' as a mechanism through which they monitor closely and track the progress of major, big-ticket projects or schemes that they are keen to push.

Similarly, the performance of a leader becomes important in the implementation of policies and programmes by the bureaucratic system. It is not enough for a politician at the helm to direct the bureaucracy to implement people-friendly policies and programmes; the political leader has to follow it to

---

[23]Sanyal, Prasad, '58-Crore Deal between DLF and Robert Vadra Cancelled by IAS Officer Ashok Khemka', *NDTV*, 16 October 2012, https://bit.ly/3JSm2SK. Accessed on 6 February 2023.

[24]Express News Service, 'Ashok Khemka Transferred for 54th Time in 29 Yrs', *The Indian Express*, 23 October 2021, https://bit.ly/3RQDXeV. Accessed on 6 February 2023.

its logical end. He has to use the carrot-and-stick approach to make the babus function, constantly monitoring and keeping the bureaucracy on its toes.

If a leader's mind space is filled with self-interest or the interests of the family, the follow-up will also be done accordingly, and the bureaucracy will get the message that its political master is more concerned with petty gains. It is rightly said that when the cat is away, the mouse will play. If the leader keeps himself away from day-to-day issues that impact the common man or is less than adequately committed to his political role, the bureaucracy around him will take matters into its own hands. The babu will have a field day, twisting and turning implementation according to his whims and fancies. Assorted representatives, from MLAs and MPs down to block-level elected representatives, will then begin to serve their personal interests and the interests of their family ecosystems.

On the other hand, if the political leader at the helm is focussed, determined and committed, and his actions follow his words, then the bureaucracy will have no choice but to fall in line. Take the example of the Modi dispensation. The Prime Minister is said to have not taken a single vacation since he assumed charge in 2014, and as a result, his ministers have followed suit, by and large. Once a Union minister sought leave to go abroad for a personal trip in May 2015. He was asked to tender his resignation before he proceeded for his trip. He got the message and promptly withdrew the leave request! Early on in his tenure, Modi is said to have called up ministers on their office phones at 9.30 a.m. only to check if they have reached the office or not. Not surprisingly, such steps have kept his ministers and bureaucrats on their toes.

A political party cannot survive on just slogans or ideology. It needs money. Funds come from various sources—from the common man to the wealthy and well-connected, and from individuals to corporates. But since there is no such thing as a free lunch, it is important for a political leader to keep in mind the compromises that are being made or have to be made in lieu of such money. Is the money adding value to the organization or the individual political leader, or is it leading to an unacceptable compromise? If the leader does not have clarity, problems can arise later, and these problems can lead to the government's downfall.

Bureaucrats observe such developments with a keen eye. The senior echelons of the bureaucracy are, after all, the cream of society—intelligent, shrewd and well-informed. A political leader must have the required stature to handle the bureaucracy effectively, else he runs the risk of being taken for a ride.

What makes it so crucial for leaders to have a grip on the bureaucracy is that a free rein to bureaucrats is also unhealthy for a vibrant democracy. Unlike politicians, who have to face electoral tests every five years, bureaucrats don't necessarily have to face public accountability, nor are they answerable to the people the way that elected public representatives are. For a leader to be effective, he should have a good understanding of how systems and the bureaucracy function. First-time leaders should be trained on how to effectively manage bureaucrats.

A good example of this is the state of our education system. Despite having primary education to be free-of-cost through government facilities, the private education sector is mushrooming in the country. The reason is simple: the quality of government schools is far from satisfactory. This is, despite government teachers being recruited and paid more.

The quality of primary education in government schools has deteriorated over the decades as vested interests ensured this to help private schools flourish.

The need to be effective in tackling the bureaucracy is even more urgent, since it is for the political leadership to determine which bureaucrat is best suited to promote his and his party's interests. Because most bureaucrats have considerable work experience at the grassroots level, they are equipped for all sorts of policy and programme implementation. The intent of the political leader is critical here. The choice of a wrong bureaucrat can mar governance.

Even within leaders, dynasts are often unable to manage a grip over bureaucracy because they have such little exposure to ground realities. So, bureaucrats can take such leaders for a ride, or simply refuse to execute the leaders' priorities if it doesn't suit them, by giving a variety of excuses. Dynasts, often, can do little but quibble. On the other hand, leaders who have emerged from the grassroots are generally headstrong and hard-boiled and don't give in easily when bureaucrats try and decline their legitimate requests, or obfuscates them.

A former railway minister, a political strongman, was so headstrong when he was convinced on matters that he would get bureaucrats within the ministry to move swiftly and process the proposal in record speed, and not allow any official to delay it without reasons. What matters here the most is the leader's intent.

Take the example of Uttar Pradesh. Law and order have always been a priority for the Yogi Adityanath government, and this is understandable since the state has had a reputation under the regimes of other parties for being lawless. The Yogi government has, therefore, been specially focussed on getting the right bureaucrats and police officials at the helm to handle law and order, constantly reshuffling officers in important positions. Interestingly, the BJP government there had fought both the 2017 and 2022 Assembly Elections by keeping the issue of law and order in focus—the first time it did so by pointing to lawlessness in earlier regimes, and in 2022, it presented its report card on the issue and sought votes.

Thus, the intent of the leader leads to the selection of the right officer for the right place. It's like a dispenser—you press 'Pepsi' and you get just that; you choose a Coke and you get Coke. The intent is what matters.

There is an important need for bureaucrats to also show an intent to change. Demographics have changed, needs of people have changed and, hence, there is a need for a radical shift in the way governance is also done. Bureaucrats need to be trained and upskilled to adapt governance as per these changing times. Right training for both our leaders and bureaucrats is needed.

4

LEADER AND THE ORGANIZATION

If politics has an equivalent of the classic chicken-and-egg conundrum, it is this: What comes first, a strong leader or a robust organization? In other words, does a leader owe his prominence to the political organization he belongs, or does an organization survive, even thrive, primarily because of its leader? The question may appear to be rhetorical, but in its answer lies the key to the success of leaders and political parties.

It's a tricky balance to achieve. An over-dependence on leaders can throttle the organizational growth of parties. On the other hand, a party with a robust organizational base but lacking a credible face can also suffer, if the voters are left confused over who will lead the government when the party comes to power.

For instance, in the West Bengal elections of May 2021, the BJP was locked in a fierce battle with the powerful Trinamool Congress (TMC). While the TMC had Chief Minister Mamata Banerjee leading from the front, the BJP did not have any credible face to project as an alternative to her, even though the party had been building its organizational base in the state gradually. The results made the difference clear: The TMC won three times the number of seats the BJP got. Hence, it is important for all parties to get the leadership–organization mix right.

We can approach the issue with the examples of both national and regional parties, as well as family-driven and people-centric. The BJP and the prominent Left parties are cadre-oriented and people-driven parties. While they have prominent leaders in their midst, most of these leaders have risen from the grassroots through the ranks. They owe their prominence to the masses and to the organization that has helped them gain their positions. This is why these parties have had the strength to bounce back from defeats and occupy pole positions in the country's electoral space.

The BJP had just two MPs in the Lok Sabha in 1984 but became the first party in 30 years to gain a majority on its own, in 2014; it followed up the achievement five years later with an even bigger number. The Left Front, which came to power in West Bengal after displacing the Congress party, thereafter ruled for close to 30 years without a break before being eased out—not by the Congress, but by one of its breakaway factions, the TMC.

While it is true that the success of the BJP and the TMC was due to certain tall leaders—Vajpayee, Advani and thereafter Narendra Modi for the BJP and Mamata Banerjee for the TMC—it was the party's robust organizational base that fetched the results. Without an organization that is well-oiled to take the message of the party's leaders across the masses, there is little prospect of success.

For instance, even though much of the credit for the BJP's success in the 2014 Lok Sabha polls has gone to Narendra

Modi and his campaigning skills, the truth is that without the army of the BJP's dedicated workers down to the booth level and the RSS cadre, such a scale of success would not have been possible.

On the other hand, the Congress party has depended almost entirely on the Nehru–Gandhi family for its sustenance and leadership. As a result, instead of building the organization, the party has focussed on propping up the Nehru–Gandhi leadership and accruing loyalty points with its 'high command'. Not surprisingly, it has ceded political space to its rivals, the BJP and a clutch of regional outfits, over the years.

This had not always been the case. During Nehru's time and even in the earlier years of Indira Gandhi's leadership, the Congress party's organization played a determining role in the advancement of electoral prospects. However, as the party's culture increasingly focussed inwards, i.e., on the Nehru–Gandhis, more than outwards, on its organization and the party's growth, the party's affairs went downhill. From being in power for two consecutive terms in New Delhi, the Congress party lost two Lok Sabha elections, not even managing to get enough seats to qualify as the main opposition. Not just that, the Congress has lost a string of assembly elections—a trend that continued at the time of writing this book.

When parties give primacy either to an individual or to a family, the organization at the grassroots tends to become weak. The crisis is compounded when selected, rather than elected, leaders occupy key organizational posts at the national, state, district and block levels. These leaders focus on appeasing the leadership that 'selected' them rather than workers or voters who 'elected' them. As a result, dedicated workers get demoralized, realizing that they have no future in a party whose top leadership believes in rewarding a select group of people and thereby ignoring the claims of those who may be more meritorious but not as close to the leadership or without the dynast tag. They then begin to drift away, and those that remain become inactive. Today, the Congress finds it difficult to get good candidates to contest elections in politically crucial states such as Uttar Pradesh and Bihar because the organization in those states has been virtually ground to dust.

We have also seen in recent months a trend of even leaders close to the Nehru–Gandhis getting disenchanted and quitting the party. The reason is that they grasped the reality of the Congress failing to reinvent itself according to current needs.

Similarly, the Congress is struggling to remain relevant in other electorally big states too, such as West Bengal, Odisha and Andhra Pradesh, where it once reigned supreme. In Tamil Nadu, it depends on the regional DMK, in Karnataka, on the Janata Dal (Secular) or JD(S) and so on. Its organization has been all but wiped out in Jammu and Kashmir because of its over-dependence on the regional party, the National Conference. More recently, it has suffered a major setback with the departure of its senior leader and its most prominent face in Jammu and Kashmir, Ghulam Nabi Azad, who has made it his mission to add more miseries to the party he once belonged to. Azad's departure has given the lesson that the party has only lost the plot but is also not heeding the advice of its senior leaders who have worked at the grassroots and held important organizational positions for decades.

In Maharashtra, barring the Vidarbha region, the party does not have a strong presence, and from being the dominant partner till a decade ago, has been forced to play second fiddle to its ally, the NCP, to remain in circulation. This is ironical because the NCP, although a breakaway faction of the Congress, is now the major player in the state as compared to the Congress.

In Maharashtra, a roll call of the party's leaders shows just what ails it—being dominated by second-generation dynasts, elected mostly from family strongholds; from Varsha Gaikwad, the daughter of former MP Eknath Gaikwad; Amit Deshmukh, the elder son of the late Chief Minister Vilasrao Deshmukh; to Praneeti Shinde, daughter and political heir of the former Union Home Minister Sushilkumar Shinde. Such reliance on dynasts has come at the cost of withering away of its organizational strength. In the 2019 Vidhan Sabha elections, it finished last among the major parties in Maharashtra, with just 44 seats.

A similar organizational crisis can be seen in regional parties that have their foundations in caste and religion politics. Take the example of the SP in Uttar Pradesh and the RJD in Bihar. Both rely on the Yadav vote bank, and coupled with the Muslim votes, they have often succeeded in elections. However, this has also had a negative impact at the organizational level. The non-Yadav workers at the grassroots know that their prospects of rising high are dim, and, therefore, they seek other avenues. Both the RJD and the SP have lost ground because their organizations have failed to honour the sentiments and aspirations of those workers who come from non-Yadav backgrounds.

The BSP is another case in point. When Kanshi Ram founded the party, he brought a rainbow of Scheduled Castes (SCs), STs and OBCs into the party fold, thus ensuring the support of all these sections. However, over the years, with Mayawati at the helm, the BSP became a party of the Dalits, while the others were sidelined. The result is there for everyone to see.

Why would the foot soldiers remain attached to parties in which they do not have a future simply because they do not have the right caste affiliation? If a party is in power, perhaps such foot soldiers will hang on for a while because of the benefits that come with being on the side of the ruler. But no sooner the party loses power, the ignored grassroots workers and leaders will dump it and go wherever they find themselves welcome. Over the past few years, the family-driven Congress, the National Conference and the Peoples Democratic Party (PDP) have lost many of its prominent faces to other parties after ceding power.

The foot soldiers of such parties ask, and with some justification: Why should I work in the way my leaders want me to, when I am ignored? There must be some incentive that the leader or the party has to offer. Foot soldiers remain attached to a party either because of tangible and intangible benefits—from wider clout to financial rewards—or because they share a bond with their leaders.

Unless you have a party leader who treats you like family or an important element of the organization, you will not extend loyalty beyond a point, and that bond will not exist. It is the duty of a leader to keep the workers feeling wanted. In a small party, loyalty is easy to maintain since the leader can manage personal contacts with their workers. But as the party grows and expands, it is not easy to maintain such contacts. The problem is taken care of when there is an organization that offers opportunities to the foot soldiers on multiple fronts, in the form of leadership positions at state and local levels.

If an organization believes only in the family, and the family surname matters above everything else, why will the cadre that does not belong to that surname work for the organization? At the individual level, if the leader prioritizes their own family, gives them major posts and preference for important roles, the worker has nothing to feel incentivized with. The SP's best strike rate on its own is around 30 per cent of votes polled in Uttar Pradesh. The same is the case for the RJD in Bihar. Most of these votes come from the Yadav community and the Muslim voters. It is taken for granted by the cadre of these parties that they will not get anything if they are not from the Yadav community.

Neglect of the organization can also happen in parties that may not be family-driven but are individual-centric to such an extent that the person rather than the party becomes primary. The BSP and the All India Anna Dravida Munnetra Kazhagam (AIADMK) serve as good examples of that. In the first case, it is Mayawati, and in the second, it was M.G. Ramachandran in the beginning and J. Jayalalithaa later. The AIADMK is today struggling politically in the absence of Jayalalithaa. There are at least three factions of the party that splintered after her death, and are in the middle of a fractious dispute to wrest control of the party. All through Jayalalithaa's tenure, the party organization was an extension of her own persona, with no nurturing of second- and third-rung leadership. The vacuum created by her death could not be filled because there was nobody from the organization who could rise to that stature, even when they got an opportunity. The BSP is facing a similar decline after its supremo Mayawati's loss of sheen since 2014.

But it is not just the regional parties or the Congress that face the failure of the leadership brand to influence electoral results. The BJP too has struggled with the challenge in southern states such as Kerala, Tamil Nadu, Andhra Pradesh, Telangana and, to an extent, Karnataka. In all these states, as in others, the Modi brand is known. But it has not worked in the BJP's favour because the party does not have the deep organization required in those states to exploit that brand equity.

This can be understood by the following corporate example. 'X' is a nationally known detergent brand and has the maximum market share across the country. But it is not easily available in certain parts, and thus, the consumers in those parts adopt a different brand. Visibility is important, and in the political context, visibility comes via the organization and its leaders at the grassroots levels.

Amidst all this, Odisha Chief Minister Naveen Patnaik stands out as a stark contrast. His political journey offers food for thought. He began his tenure as the son of the stalwart politician Biju Patnaik, and his acceptability level was not very high on his own individual merit. But as he progressed in his role, he was able to shrug off the family baggage and emerge as a political leader in his own right. Today, he does not have to invoke his family name to seek votes; he gets them through his performance as chief minister, and with the help of an organization, which, though established by his father, was expanded and strengthened by him.

When family or individual interests take a higher importance than an organization's interests, the immediate hit is directly taken by the party. But in the mid- and long-term, the top leadership is also impacted. When that happens, the leadership gets weakened. It does not end there—an emaciated leadership offers a fertile ground for various influential party men to promote their own vested interests. The organization becomes a vehicle for the implementation of individual agendas that are not always beneficial to the party. Sincere and able leaders, perceiving that the top leadership is busy with promoting their own interests, get frustrated and rebel.

We saw that happen to the Congress party in Madhya Pradesh, when Jyotiraditya Scindia, sidelined by the state leadership and having failed in his efforts to convince the party's high command about his continuing humiliation, quit the party in disgust and joined the BJP. Not just that, he had enough supporters in the assembly who were equally enraged, ready to bring down the Congress government of Kamal Nath and install a BJP regime in its place.

Nothing illustrates this better than the events of June 2022 in Maharashtra. Shiv Sena, the strong regional party founded by the late chief Bal Thackeray, was wracked by rebellions across its ranks, with a majority of its MLAs and MPs deserting the party despite the party's chief, Uddhav Thackeray, being the chief minister. In the days after the revolt, some of these reasons behind the rebellion were revealed. They were all too similar to what I mentioned above—the party leaders accused Thackeray of promoting his son Aaditya and other members of his family, and being closeted with a group of loyalists and not remaining accessible to others. Frustrated at Thackeray making clear who his heir is and his ignoring of others, senior leaders in the party wondered what their future would be in such a party, and they rebelled against him. The lessons here apply to many a political dynast across the country.

Almost a similar revolt brewed in Congress-ruled Rajasthan with Sachin Pilot leading the band of rebels. But the Ashok Gehlot government survived because the numerical gap between his supporting MLAs and those in the rebel camp was too high for Pilot to bridge.

However, the final word is yet to be had, with differences continuing to simmer. While it is true that the differences between Scindia and Kamal Nath went back several years, matters came to a boil after the party high command, itself weakened as a result of successive assembly and Lok Sabha defeats, failed to contain the situation.

Eventually, everything boils down to man-management. Simply put, it is about handling the organization. The BJP emerged from the Bharatiya Jana Sangh, which was a grassroots-driven party. Its leaders rose through the ranks. The Congress too was an outcome of a people's movement and remained people-driven for some years, but the degeneration began after it turned into a family affair from the mid-1970s.

For the BJP, Amit Shah is the perfect man-manager, not only plotting the party's election campaigns with the help of his connect with leaders from the top to the grassroots, but also building strategic coalitions with allies in the Northeast and elsewhere. Another good example is the NCP chief Sharad Pawar. When the Sudhakarrao Naik-led Congress government came under attack after the 1993 terror strike in Maharashtra, the Congress party turned to a young Pawar, then in the party, to assume charge of the state. He was able to quell internal dissent and restore a sense of stability in governance. More recently, he was instrumental in creating the Maha Vikas Aghadi coalition in the state with the Shiv Sena as an unlikely partner, along with the Congress—and forming a government.

A leader's connection with and understanding of people thus matters enough to make a difference between winning and losing. His word should be respected and agreed upon.

That is the mark of a seasoned leader. Such a leader knows which issues can trigger a crisis and which can bring matters under control. For those like Pawar, family is important, but the organization is equally so. They realize the fact that if the family fails the organization, the organization too will fail the family. This is what has happened to the Congress party.

Pawar has been conscious of the challenges within his own family and organization and has handled them deftly. His nephew, Ajit Pawar, has been seen as a natural political heir to the Maratha strongman. But the rise of Pawar's daughter, Supriya Sule, has caused some consternation to Ajit and his loyalists. Ajit's rebellion against his uncle in 2019, when he tried to split the NCP and back the BJP in Maharashtra, should be seen in this light. But Pawar has tried to keep the spheres of influence of both Ajit and his daughter Supriya mutually exclusive. While Ajit remains the senior-most leader in state politics after Pawar, Sule remains active in national politics, as the party's face in New Delhi. This way, Pawar has tried to separate their domains, and thereby reduce points of friction.

But party insiders believe that this might not be enough: The NCP's future, post Pawar, remains as yet unclear. Nonetheless, Pawar has also taken care to cultivate a strong second-rung leadership, with a battery of senior leaders at the state level, who are instrumental in shaping all major decisions in the party.

A good leader should also be able to deal with situations—within family, within the party and within the bureaucracy and government—when in power. The challenge becomes greater once a leader is elected to a post, even if it is as an MP or MLA. Pressures from party men and from family members begin to mount. A poor leader, especially one who does not have a mass base, will find it difficult to handle the situation. If he has nothing to offer to his people because he himself is at the mercy of somebody else, or has only the family name to offer, he loses his shine. Desertions thereafter begin.

Right from the ancient times of 'Raja–Praja', India has always preferred to follow the concept of dynastic rule. Even in 1947, Mahatma Gandhi virtually announced Jawaharlal Nehru as the prime minister of independent India till the time the first elections happened in 1952, and the tradition followed from there.

Dynastic rule is against the basic principles of a democracy. In political dynasticism, more than the country and its people, the interests of the family and associates are given preference—just like what a king used to do for his relatives and clan. The philosophy of Chanakya (*kutniti*) might have been relevant in that age when the basic aim of any king was to expand his kingdom. Even today, politicians fight within and outside the party for extension of power and adopt the tactics of kutniti; but in reality, if they want to succeed, they have to just go with what people want.

The basic principle of ruling needs to change as we celebrate 75 years of our Independence. The penchant to be a 'pradhan sevak' is seen in no politician except a few, like Narendra Modi and Naveen Patnaik. A leader and his organization both need to change to keep up with the times.

~

5

THE GAME OF ALTERNATIVES

In May 1980, British Prime Minister Margaret Thatcher addressed a Conservative Party's women's conference and, pushing for a balance in production and earning, said:

> There is no easy popularity in what we are proposing but it is fundamentally sound. Yet I believe people accept there is no real alternative... What's the alternative? To go on as we were before? All that leads to is higher spending... And that means more taxes, more borrowings, higher interest rates, more inflation, more unemployment.[25]

The speech became memorable because of a key phrase that soon became the acronym TINA: There Is No (real) Alternative. The 'TINA' factor is a term that is now employed across domains, not just in the context of economics that Thatcher used.

In politics, this can often be the most crucial element—

[25]'Speech to Conservative Women's Conference', Margaret Thatcher Foundation, 21 May 1980, https://bit.ly/3m0KlnO

the 'X' factor—that can swing one's fortune and make the difference between a loser and a winner. But in the world's largest democracy, a country with over 5,000 registered and unregistered political parties and a vibrant, raucous political scene, can it ever be the case that there is really no alternative to some individual or some party?

As I have written before, voters make a rational choice generally in casting their vote and choosing a person or party based on a number of parameters. But their evaluation of the person or party on these parameters is influenced, primarily, by their perception. This perception is, in turn, based, among other things, on that person or party's performance. The voters' perception, accurate or otherwise, of how a leader has performed or will potentially perform in the future, if elected, dictates their voting pattern.

Ahead of the 2019 Lok Sabha polls, journalist Kunal Purohit, reporting from Jharkhand for IndiaSpend, wrote about a small hamlet of Dalit Malhars, who had been displaced from their original homes by local villagers.[26] Most of the Malhar community members were far away from accessing government schemes—most did not even have ration cards. So, none of them were in a position to vote for the Modi government on the basis of its welfare benefits, since they had received none. Yet, Purohit found that villagers were supporting Modi and wanted to back him. The reason was that they believed he was best placed to improve their lives in the future. This is how perception influences people's voting choices.

---

[26]Purohit, Kunal, 'In Backward Regions of a Backward State, Modi Is the Choice', *IndiaSpend*, 27 April 2019, https://bit.ly/3JHRZ0h. Accessed on 6 February 2023.

This was, for them, the belief that there was no real alternative to Modi, as far as their well-being was concerned. No one was better placed than him to deliver better governance than what they had been subjected to.

The TINA factor, therefore, does not mean that there are no alternatives in the absolute sense. In the village in Jharkhand mentioned above, voters had the option to vote for numerous parties—from local alternatives, regional outfits to even national rivals of the BJP, like the Congress. But for the voter, if the alternative is not credible enough, it isn't really an alternative to count on. This lack of a credible alternative has been a dominant factor in India's politics and has shaped independent India's political journey immensely.

Jawaharlal Nehru remained in power from 1947 till his death in May 1964. He was a popular prime minister, no doubt, but even when his leadership came to be questioned on a variety of issues, the voters returned him to power. The reason was not that they were deeply satisfied with his performance, but that there was no credible alternative to him. There were the Left parties and the Bharatiya Jana Sangh. But their influence was limited to a few regions and demographics in the country. Besides, they did not have a leader who could match Nehru's charisma. The voters, even when they were unhappy with the present state of affairs, had no choice but to return Nehru to office.

It is the perception that a leader creates in the minds of voters that makes them believe that there is no other alternative. Even in Nehru's times, when he was clearly the tallest leader around, American journalist Welles Hangen wrote a book busting this myth of invincibility. The 1962 book titled *After Nehru, Who?*[27] imagines a post-Nehru India where Hangen lists out eight potential successors from across the political spectrum: Morarji Desai, Krishna Menon, Lal Bahadur Shastri, Y.B. Chavan, S.K. Patil, Jayaprakash Narayan and Indira Gandhi. But this was lost to the voters, who kept thinking that the country did not really have an alternative to Nehru.

A similar situation prevailed when Indira Gandhi assumed power. The political challenges that she faced were more internal (within the party) than external (by rival parties). But for the voters, there was no real alternative to her, and so, she and her government continued to be elected. In the run-up to the 1977 general elections in the backdrop of Emergency, things changed. Jayaprakash Narayan had emerged as a magnet for opposition leaders and he had managed to bring together various leaders with different ideological leanings under one umbrella—the Janata Party. Many factors coalesced—there was fatigue with the Congress since it had ruled for three decades; the Prime Minister had grown unpopular; and the voters, now, finally got what they believed was a credible alternative. They opted for it. Indira Gandhi's party lost; she herself was defeated in her Lok Sabha constituency.

In the 1979–80 elections, the voters again had a choice—repeat the reign of the Janata Party or return to the Congress led by Indira Gandhi. The Janata Party had imploded; it had frittered away the opportunity the voters had given it and had provided poor governance. The masses voted the Congress back to power, considering it as a better alternative with Indira Gandhi at the helm.

---

[27]Hangen, Welles, *After Nehru, Who?*, Harcourt, Brace & World, 1962.

But after Indira Gandhi's assassination, Rajiv Gandhi's assumption of prime ministership and his rocky tenure marked by controversial decisions, as well as the split in the party, ensured that the lack of alternatives did not come into play. Voters had grown tired of his rule just a few years into his term. Plus, there was a credible challenger in V.P. Singh, a leader who had emerged out of the Congress itself. In the 1989 Lok Sabha elections, the voters had a choice between the Congress party and the V.P. Singh-led JD, and they chose the latter, albeit by a small margin.

The collapse of the V.P. Singh government and the splintering of parties that followed, resulted in a curious situation where the voters had far too many options to choose from. The problem, however, was one of credibility. When Thatcher meant she had 'no real alternative', she meant that while there were obvious alternatives to her economic plans, they weren't any other credible or effective alternatives to choose from. Similarly, while there were many parties to choose from in India at that time, the voters struggled to identify a credible political alternative.

The last assembly election in Punjab provided a strange version of TINA. The Congress party was in power, and had traditionally been a strong player in the state's politics. However, it decided to self-destruct just before the elections, with infighting breaking out. In the process, it deleted itself from the list of choices that the voters had. With the Shiromani Akali Dal on the back foot and the BJP not having any major presence, the AAP moved quickly to fill the vacuum. The Congress party, by its folly, had created TINA, and the beneficiary was the AAP. Thus, the TINA factor can be a mysterious element; on paper, there may be many options, but if voters don't find any one of them to be good enough, the list is redundant.

Something similar happened in the 1991 Lok Sabha polls, where the voters gave the Congress party the largest number of seats, reinforcing this factor.

That the electorate was not quite comfortable with the choice it had made was evident in the number it gave to the Congress party—244 seats, less than a simple majority. The BJP, although it had strengthened itself over the years, was still not considered a credible alternative by the voters, and it ended up with half the number of seats the Congress party got.

Five years later, the situation had changed. The BJP won 160 seats while the Congress got 20 less. This phase was marked less by the lack of a challenger, but more by a sense of confusion among voters over who deserves their vote—neither of the alternatives felt credible enough. But from 1999 to mid-2004, the BJP managed, with the help of its allies, to rule the country (with two short breaks), with Atal Bihari Vajpayee as the prime minister. The BJP may still not have got a clear majority, but it was the party with the largest number of seats and had begun to be seen as a credible alternative, even though the bulk of the BJP's seats came from the Hindi-speaking states.

With the TINA factor no longer at play, the 2004 elections witnessed a near direct contest between the BJP and the Congress party nationwide. Although the Vajpayee government was perceived to have done fairly well across all sectors and it sought to advertise its achievements through the 'India Shining' electoral campaign, the voters had other ideas. They opted for the Congress party but did not give it a majority. The interesting part is that they considered the

Congress favourably although it did not even have a prime ministerial face.

Manmohan Singh's first term as prime minister was average at best. In 2008, a year before the next elections were due, the global economic meltdown hit the country hard. The 26/11 terror strike further dented the government and the party's image. It seemed that all was lost for the Congress party. Even the United Progressive Alliance (UPA) as an alliance was seen struggling; the biggest partner, the Left Front, had withdrawn its support and the government narrowly survived a trust vote, amid allegations of trying to bribe its way to victory.

The UPA felt like a sinking ship as it faced the 2009 elections. But when the results came, they did not reflect the expected doom. The UPA won, and the Congress won even more seats than it had in 2004. Among other things, its decision to bring in the MGNREGA swung the elections decisively.

The choice before the voters in 2009 was between the BJP, led by L.K. Advani, and the Congress, helmed by Manmohan Singh. Having rejected the Vajpayee government, the voters did not feel that the Advani-led BJP was a better option. Therefore, despite anti-incumbency and an average performance, the Congress emerged as the largest party. But just five years later, things would dramatically change with the arrival of Narendra Modi on the national stage.

Until a year before the 2014 General Election, it appeared that the Congress party, in the absence of a credible alternative, could win a third term in office. There was of course the BJP, led by the experienced Advani. But Advani's leadership had been rejected by the voters in 2004 and then again in 2009, and nothing had changed since then to suggest that he had won the people's heart and mind. Besides, he had been around in national politics for so long that he lacked the novelty factor.

The BJP needed something new and refreshing by way of leadership to take on the ruling Congress party. To emerge as an option, the BJP had to clearly differentiate that it had a distinct vision and was better placed than the Congress to take the country ahead. The new leader also had to present before the people a legacy of performance, and he had to provide a striking contrast to the incumbent prime minister, Manmohan Singh.

Modi ticked all the right boxes. He had been chief minister of Gujarat since the end of 2001, and since then had been elected every time the state had gone to polls. His governance had brought about a dramatic transformation in Gujarat—something that was acknowledged not just nationally but also across the world. He is charismatic and a powerful orator, speaking a language that the masses connected with. Once he was formally announced as the BJP's prime ministerial candidate for the 2014 polls, the voters had a real, credible alternative to the Congress and Manmohan Singh. The TINA factor that had helped the Congress in 2004 and 2009 would not be operational in 2014.

If the presence or the absence of a credible alternative has directly impacted national elections, the same is equally true of state polls. Let's take the example of Tamil Nadu. Since 1969, the people of the state have voted for either the DMK or the AIADMK. This lack of alternatives has played out fully in the state. Thus, despite both parties having routinely demonstrated lack of good governance, they have been voted to power. Neither the Congress party—which was once dominant in the state—nor the BJP has, in the last half a century, been seen as a credible alternative to these regional parties. Modi's nationwide popularity has fetched no rewards for the BJP in Tamil Nadu.

In West Bengal, it was first the Congress party and then the Left Front that dominated the state politics. None could be said to have provided good governance in a sustained manner, and yet they returned to power. The Left Front ruled for close to 30 years at a stretch, but not due to the governance it delivered. It was the result of a lack of a credible alternative.

The alternative emerged in Mamata Banerjee when she took on the Left Front government aggressively in 2008 over the irregularities in the acquisition of farmlands for the Tata Nano factory in the Singur area of Nandigram in the state. She became the face of the agitation and forced the mighty Left government, not accustomed to a strong oppositional figure, to roll back its plans and cancel the acquisition process. Banerjee managed to change public perception in the state. Three years later, voters agreed that she was a credible alternative to the Left and rewarded her with a full majority. She became the chief minister, breaking down the Left's citadel.

In the decade that she has been in office, her government has fallen short on a number of parameters but has still been voted back to power. The only explanation is the absence of a credible alternative before the voters. The Left has been ground to dust, while the BJP's attempts to emerge as an option has suffered setbacks—the last one in 2021. Two years before that, in the 2019 Lok Sabha elections, the voters of the state discovered a re-energized BJP as a national option, and gave it 18 seats out of 42, but gave it the thumbs down in the state polls.

Politically, the most important—sending 80 members to the Lok Sabha—the state of Uttar Pradesh offers a good example of how this lack of alternatives works, and so does its reversal. From the mid-1990s until 2017, the people of the state voted for either the SP or the BSP to power in the assembly. National parties such as the Congress and the BJP, although present at the grassroots across the state, were not considered as credible alternatives by the voters. As a consequence, although both the regional outfits provided patchy governance and their reigns were marked by corruption, communalism and law and order issues, they returned to rule by turn.

This changed in 2017 when the BJP, riding on its 2014 Lok Sabha victory—where it had won 73 out of 80 Lok Sabha seats in Uttar Pradesh alongside its allies—recorded a decisive win in the Assembly Elections. With Yogi Adityanath as the surprise choice for the chief minister, the party went from strength to strength, winning the 2022 Assembly Elections with a clear majority as well. The choice before the people was clear: Yogi versus SP's Akhilesh Yadav or BSP's Mayawati. The voters went by performance and the tainted legacy of the leaders of the two regional parties. The Uttar Pradesh example showed that when people have a credible alternative, they do not hesitate to dump even those they have favoured for decades.

Bihar also offers a similar case. For long, the RJD led by Lalu Prasad Yadav ruled the state, with the people voting it to power despite its record of poor governance and favouritism of a certain section of the people. The voters had no credible alternatives before them. When that alternative came in the form of Nitish Kumar and his party, the Janata Dal (United) or JD(U)—backed by the BJP—the voters promptly switched sides. Nitish Kumar had a halo; he had earned the name of 'Sushasan Babu' (good governance man). Even when he tied up with the RJD, the new alliance triumphed over the BJP primarily because his stature and reputation diluted the negatives of Lalu's party. His return to the National Democratic Alliance (NDA) fold, led by the BJP, did nothing to reduce his stature.

More recently, Nitish Kumar switched back to an alliance with the RJD, dumping the BJP. But his image has taken a beating due to the frequent switchovers, and it remains to be seen if he can continue to be a force either in the state or nationally, in the months to come.

Another interesting example is that of Odisha. Naveen Patnaik, who came to power in 1997, is perceived to have given a semblance of good governance, based on which he has been repeatedly elected to power. Year after year, Odisha witnesses the nature's fury, as cyclones keeps ravaging the state. To add to it, one in every three persons in Odisha is poor. But be it cyclones or poverty, the people of Odisha vouch for how Naveen Patnaik has stood like a shield, protecting them from devastating cyclones and other natural disasters; he is not just a politician but a 'father figure' in his state. And, hence, neither Modi's stature and charisma nor the BJP's efforts at denting Patnaik's citadel have worked, either in the Lok Sabha or the assembly elections.

Patnaik managed to come out of the shadow of his father, the tall Odisha politician Biju Patnaik, but there are many others who have failed to do so. For instance, both Akhilesh Yadav and Tejashwi Yadav continue to be hounded by the baggage of their fathers' political careers. For instance, political rivals continue to target Tejashwi over the issue of 'Jungle Raj', a term that opponents used to denote the law and order situation in the years under his father Lalu Prasad Yadav's tenure as the chief minister. The fire of that allegation now singes Nitish Kumar too, as the RJD's ally.

Delhi offers a unique example. Here, Arvind Kejriwal became the chief minister once the AAP stormed to power with 67 out of 70 seats in 2015. He had no baggage, but also nothing to show by way of performance, being a first-time chief minister (if one discounts the short period when he became chief minister with the Congress's help). The BJP had been out of power for long in Delhi, with the Congress party led by Sheila Dikshit ruling the roost. It had ceased to be a credible alternative for the voters electing a local government despite the fact that it had won all the seven Lok Sabha seats in 2014 (a feat that would repeat in 2019). With the AAP winning a second term, it became clear that when the people do not have a credible alternative, they tend to repeat the incumbent, even if they have areas of dissatisfaction with the rulers.

When voters don't quite know who, between the incumbent and the challenger, is more credible, it can result in a hung assembly or Parliament. But when they do, the voters can be decisive about their choices.

6

IT'S NOT ALL ABOUT MONEY

Subject experts of economy, and even political commentators, often remark that the performance of an incumbent government, in tackling the economy of the country or a state, has a direct bearing on the results of elections. The claim, however, is not supported by factual data, at least in the Indian context.

First, some recent evidence. The pandemic and the lockdowns across the country wreaked havoc on people's livelihoods and, consequently, inflicted heavy economic toll on the country's fiscal health. Unemployment skyrocketed, the country's gross domestic product (GDP) nosedived, and any improvement seemed far away. Yet, this hasn't really extracted a political cost from the BJP, which is ruling at the Centre and is in charge of safeguarding the country's fiscal wealth. In fact, in the 12 states that have seen polls since the lockdown of March 2020, the BJP has not lost even a single state where it was ruling. Surely, if the country's economic health was at the top of voters' minds, the BJP would have felt the repercussions of these concerns.

For more than three decades, between the 1950s and the

1980s, the average growth of GDP was in the range of just 3.5 per cent. The per capita income grew by only 1.3 per cent. Noted economist Raj Krishna allegedly termed it as the 'Hindu rate of growth',[28] which rested on *karma* and *bhagya* (fortune). Yet, the governments of, first Pandit Jawaharlal Nehru and later Indira Gandhi, remained dominant players, nearly unshakeable and earning repeated runs.

As prime minister, Narasimha Rao embarked on the first genuine economic reforms programme in 1991, backed ably by his finance minister, Manmohan Singh. In one stroke of the pen, so to say, the Rao government dismantled the decades-old licence-permit-quota raj system and brought in several measures to liberalize the Indian economy, including a new industrial policy. Although he was a Congress member, heavily influenced by socialism, Rao showed remarkable courage in junking the supposedly socialist economic policies that successive governments since Independence had followed.

He faced a moment of reckoning similar to what British Prime Minister Margaret Thatcher had faced when she made her famous 'there is no real alternative' remark. Rao had inherited a broken economy and the only fix was a major surgery. The country had foreign reserves that were barely enough to pay for two weeks of imports; his predecessor had to pledge the country's gold to raise money from the International Monetary Fund (though even that amount was not sufficient to tide over the looming crisis). The economy had to be opened up; private enterprises had to be given prominence and even priority and the bleeding public-sector

---

[28]Siva, Meera, 'What's a "Hindu" Rate of Growth', *The Hindu*, 10 March 2018, https://bit.ly/3xicnxB. Accessed on 14 February 2023.

units had to be revamped. Rao told Manmohan Singh to go ahead with whatever was needed to bring about a dramatic transformation, and assured his full political support in any eventuality.

What happened thereafter is history. The scale and magnitude of the reforms changed the country's economic profile and became a template for future economic planning. India had been saved from economic ruin.

One would have thought that the significance of this moment would be so momentous that voters would, in appreciation of Rao and his government's bold economic steps, reward him with a second term in power, that this paradigm shift in the country's economics would drown out any other failures of the government. But Rao's government could not be saved. It lost the 1996 elections, yet again underlining the fact that the management of the economy is not a major election issue when it comes to voting choices.

A similar situation saw itself getting repeated less than a decade later. Atal Bihari Vajpayee was the first non-Congress prime minister to complete a full term, and his tenure was marked by an unprecedented emphasis on infrastructure—roads, health, education, telecommunication, etc. The economy grew between 8 and 10 per cent, and inflation was within manageable limits. By all accounts, the Vajpayee regime had managed the economy well. In fact, the buzz around the economy was so pronounced that it even goaded the BJP to go into the elections with its now-infamous 'India Shining' campaign, which focussed on the economic growth the country was seeing. Yet, Vajpayee lost.

Ten years later, this happened again. In 2014, the country's economy was in fairly good shape under Manmohan Singh's second term, but the Congress party lost the elections. A survey conducted in April 2014,[29] during the campaign for those polls, showed that voters were optimistic about the country's progress, with over 60 per cent of those surveyed, across age groups, believing that the country was doing well. A similar percentage of people believed that the country's economy was faring well and getting better. But this satisfaction with the government's economic handling did not reflect in the results of the polls—the Congress suffered its worst-ever performance, being reduced to only 44 Lok Sabha seats.

The tenuous linkage of the economy with election results has also been demonstrated in state poll results. Take the example of N. Chandrababu Naidu. As the chief minister of undivided Andhra Pradesh, he led the state to a new era of economic development. Back in the 1990s, he anticipated the growth of technology and its future role in revolutionizing governance, and put in place a massive programme to promote the information technology (IT) sector in the state. His efforts bore fruit when Hyderabad emerged as a national hotspot for the IT industry. Naidu was globally and nationally recognized for his achievements—*India Today* gave him the IT India Millennium award; *The Economic Times* made him the Business Person of the Year and he was offered a honorary professorship at Kellogg School of Management in the United States.

But, despite such lofty accolades, the Telugu Desam Party (TDP) he led lost the 2004 state elections, securing just 47

---

[29]S., Rukmini, 'How India Votes: Does It Matter What Voters Think of Modi Government's Economic Performance?', *Scroll.in*, 7 February 2019, https://bit.ly/3X3EFGw. Accessed on 6 February 2023.

of the 294 seats. The TDP under his leadership also lost the 2009 state polls. It was said that Naidu's defeat was because he had neglected the rural sector while focussing his attention on the cities.

Conversely, the Left Front continued to rule West Bengal for 34 years, despite its poor economic management. Once the hub of industry—with jute and textiles as the mainstay—West Bengal turned into a virtual industrial graveyard in the Left years, with the flight of industries and capital from the state. Until the early 1960s, the state's per capita income was higher than the national average. By the early 1980s, it dropped to the national average and then continued to fall in state rankings on the particular indicator. This fall continued with the change in government and the assumption of power by Mamata Banerjee's TMC. And yet, both the Left Front and the TMC continued to get support from the voters and got elected.

This disconnect between a government's economic performance and its winnability factor may sound strange, but it is not so if one scratches beyond the surface of the argument.

This isn't to say that voters are not bothered about the economy at all. But voters have different economic parameters in mind, distinct from the parameters that economists and economic experts have, when evaluating the economy.

In our many interactions with the people over time, the voters explain the economic factors that drive their voting behaviour. Many of them tell us how their economic well-being has benefitted from the direct transfer of benefits straight into their bank accounts or how the construction of their own house, facilitated by government subsidies through the Pradhan Mantri Awas Yojana scheme, have empowered them.

For voters, the economic health of a country is often what they see reflected around them as 'development', be it infrastructure—better roads, smoother power supply—or more government welfare schemes and less in jargon that is disconnected from their lives. Politicians realize this visualization.

The late Jayalalithaa, who ruled Tamil Nadu with an iron fist, was no economist. But under her, the voters were promised a slew of incentives during election campaigns that would make them economically stronger or, often, make their lives easier and more prosperous. Some of the freebies that Jayalalithaa offered ranged from kitchen appliances to home devices. Her pet scheme to offer subsidized cooked food, through canteens named 'Amma canteens' after her, were a big hit since poorer sections could now have hot, cooked meals at next-to-nothing prices.

As a result, successful political leaders at the Centre and the state level, be it Prime Minister Modi, Madhya Pradesh Chief Minister Shivraj Singh Chouhan or even Telangana Chief Minister K. Chandrashekhar Rao, are all investing in bringing forth innovative social welfare schemes for the large swathes of lower-middle class populations. In these states, our election surveys often reveal how these schemes have played a big part in re-electing these leaders. Voters often compare these programmes to the lack of such schemes in previous regimes, and thereby decide to re-elect these regimes and reward them with their votes.

In contrast, an economist measures growth by tracking the rise or fall of the GDP. The higher the GDP as compared to the previous period, the better the economy is considered to be performing. The economist also measures a government's performance by the levels of inflation—high inflation is bad economic management and controlled inflation is praiseworthy. The third parameter that is considered by the experts is the Sensex. If it is high, it means that investor sentiments are buoyant; if it plunges and remains low for weeks, there is something wrong that needs to be fixed. The fourth is tax collections. If the economy is doing well, tax receipts are high too.

Now, let's consider the matter from a lay voter's perspective. He couldn't be bothered with the performance of the Sensex, nor does GDP make any sense to him. Inflation is a vague concept for him; all that voters care about are the prices of the essential products that they consume. Neither the Sensex, inflation figures, GDP figures nor tax collections are high in his list of considerations when he goes to vote. Over 70 per cent of the voters are from rural India and their concerns revolve around affordable healthcare for their family, basic education for their children and other essential amenities at reasonable prices, as well as law and order. Many of these voters grow enough food grains to feed their families. If their essential needs are taken care of, they are content.

The only other thing that matters to the ordinary voter is employment. There is a link between good economic performance of the government and employment rates. However, that is more so in the developed countries than in India. The reason is that employment is heavily dependent in developed nations on a robust industrial activity. In India's case, though, that is not so. India is not a highly industrialized nation, and an overwhelming majority of its population still depends on agriculture or agriculture-related activities. But the contribution of agriculture to GDP is around just 15 per cent. Therefore, even if the GDP goes down, it makes little difference to the majority of voters.

There is yet another, rather interesting, aspect—business booms when demand goes up; and when there is an escalation in demand, prices of various products naturally go up. On the other hand, when business is down—or, when economic growth is sluggish—demand plummets, and the price of various products also witnesses a downward trend. This is good for the ordinary voter, since he gets many of his essentials at a cheaper rate! Therefore, as far as he is concerned, a poor economy is, in some respect, a blessing in disguise, and he is unlikely to punish the government only for that.

It can be argued that when economic growth is robust, it leads to higher tax collections, which in turn can be used to promote the many welfare schemes that are needed by the masses. But only a part of the taxes collected go into welfare programmes, and a dip in tax collection, thus, does not greatly impact the schemes that benefit the needy.

Finally, economic growth in terms of industrial growth is a much-hyped phenomenon in India. Only a handful of states, such as Maharashtra, Tamil Nadu, Kerala and Karnataka, have an industrial base of consequence. The rest are hardly impacted, and their voters too are less affected by a downturn in industrial activity or the economic fortunes associated with it.

To sum up, the connection between economic (or GDP) growth and electoral results is more an imagination of the experts. The reality, as the empirical data shows, is very different.

~

7

THE ROLE OF GEOGRAPHY

In his seminal work, *Revenge of Geography,* author Robert Kaplan offers a brilliant and original insight into the role of geographical locations in understanding the important pivots of history and in grasping modern-day challenges. Kaplan tries to understand the role of geography in shaping everything, from border conflicts to the growth of religion to foreign policy. Such a lens of geography is also critical when we try to look at our own country's politics and democracy.

Few realize how geographical behaviour, or behaviour shaped due to geography, is a factor that determines the way politics and, as a result, election results play out in our country. Even psephologists and expert commentators have not looked at geography close enough. But having been in this business, I can tell you this: The reason why it is so difficult to correctly predict election results is geography; the reason why a state votes overwhelmingly for a party in one contest but reduces it to rubble in the very next one, is geography; the reason why a state returns the same party to power for decades is geography; and the reason why god-men influence electoral outcomes in one region but are non-entities in another is also geography.

Let me explain. India is one entity, one composite nation and country. Yet, it houses a baffling level of diversity in every way. It is behaviourally versatile and difficult, making the task of accurately understanding the mood of the entire nation almost impossible. Voters are known to have sprung surprises, bringing in unknowns and voting out the established. The complexity from the demographic changes that characterize one geographical location from another—one state from another—adds to the difficulty of predicting elections because people of one geographical location behave in a way that is not only different from but also at times opposite of what those in another location do.

Let us consider some facts. India has nearly two dozen official languages and over a thousand dialects. If you travel across the country, you could find a new dialect every 50 km and a new language every 100 km. It has the second-highest population of English speakers in the world, and yet, less than 10 per cent of Indians can communicate in that language. It has a staggering 543 Lok Sabha constituencies, which means that voters elect 543 members to the Lower House directly through a free and fair democratic process. These constituencies are composed of voters that may be very different from one another in their choices, preferences, needs and aspirations.

As if that is not complicated enough, the demographic profile of the country has kept changing, and dramatically at that, thus making the job of understanding voting patterns that much more daunting. Take the following figures as examples. In 1950, the population was 361 million; by 2015, it was 1.2 billion. Literacy rate in the corresponding period was 18.3 per cent and 74 per cent, respectively. Life expectancy rose from a mere 36.9 years to 67.7 years in this period. All this diversity often gets reflected on the voting patterns in the country.

The country's predominant rural, agrarian nature deeply shapes its politics. The fact that 70 per cent of the country's population live in the hinterlands means that rural issues have a major bearing on the fortunes of political parties. These parties are forced to focus on agrarian issues, as well as issues of the rural masses, if they want to have a winning chance of coming to power.

Despite this uniformly agrarian nature, there is immense diversity within these areas when it comes to their voting patterns. A spatial analysis of the NDA's victory in 2019, as compared to its win in 2014, illustrated this.[30] From bagging as much as 70 per cent vote share in some northern and western states, the NDA's vote share dipped dramatically as you went south, down to as little as five per cent in some southern states.

It becomes necessary, therefore, to simplify matters, if only to get a better grip on the complexity and make sense of the astounding demographic diversity that drives electoral results. India can be geographically divided into four sections: North, South, East (including Northeast) and West. This is not merely a directional division; the characteristics which define these regions actually influence voting patterns to a large extent.

Literacy levels are different across the country. Different levels of literacy have varied social effects and, as a result, shape politics differently. The highest literacy levels and educational competence are to be found in South India. The voters of this

[30]Guilmoto, Christophe Z., 'Spatial Analysis of India's 2019 Elections Reveals the Unique Geography of the Hindu Right's Victory', *The Conversation*, 19 June 2019, https://bit.ly/3jBRVEB. Accessed on 6 February 2023.

region—including the states of Kerala, Tamil Nadu, Andhra Pradesh and Karnataka—possess a high level of political understanding and interpretational acumen.

As a result, the factors that affect voters in these regions are different from those influencing voters in areas with lower literacy levels. In many parts of the country, god-men and religious figures shape the minds of voters and urge them to vote one way or another.

But in the South, voters are not easily swayed by these god-men. The voters of the South also have a healthy disdain for political parties and leaders, as a result of which they are unwilling to extend unconditional and long-term commitment or loyalty to them. As a result, they do not have the patience or desire to keep voting for one particular party for too long.

Take the example of Tamil Nadu. We have seen that neither of the two major regional parties, the DMK and the AIADMK, that dominate the state's political landscape get to rule for more than two consecutive terms at most. Indeed, the voters bring one of these parties with a sweeping majority in one election and, five years later, reduce it to rubble. The change is decisive and there is no scope for a hung assembly.

In Kerala, too, people have voted in either the Congress party or the Left Democratic Front (LDF) by decisive margins, giving neither of the parties more than two successive terms. Pollsters confidently predict results based on the premise that a change is inevitable every five or 10 years.

In Andhra Pradesh, the Congress party, the TDP, and lately the Yuvajana Sramika Rythu Congress Party (YSRCP) have been given opportunities by way of a 'revolving door' policy. Despite his success in dramatically altering the face of Hyderabad—both in the civic sense and bringing it on the international map of information technology—N. Chandrababu Naidu led his party to a spectacular defeat, paving the way for the return of the Congress. But years later, the voters opted for the same Naidu they had decisively rejected.

A similar story is evident in the assembly results of Karnataka, where the Congress, the JD(S) and the BJP, either solely or in alliance with one or the other, have ruled in turn. In the Lok Sabha elections as well, a similar trend has been witnessed over the decades from these southern states.

Let's now consider western India, with electoral importance for the two states of Gujarat and Maharashtra. They share near similar characteristics. While the education levels of the people here are not as high as in the South, the economic indicators are better. People are more business-minded than their southern counterparts, and thus have more assured and higher means of income. This impacts their behaviour, including in the choice of parties and leaders. Since there is relatively higher economic prosperity, there are fewer tussles at interpersonal levels.

The voters are, therefore, content to give the politicians and parties the long rope and are not inclined to frequently change rulers. They value stability, including political stability. Loyalty is, thus, important. One rarely sees large-scale defections from either the Congress or the BJP or the Shiv Sena in Maharashtra, notwithstanding the political crisis that broke out in the state in June 2021, when 40 Shiv Sena legislators rebelled to pull down the Shiv Sena–NCP–Congress government in the state and, instead, backed the BJP.

Their individual vote banks are stable and largely secure, whether they are in alliance or they do it alone. We have thus seen that the vote share of the major parties remain more or less the same in all situations. Similarly, the loyalty to independent candidates is higher here than in other states of the country; independents are known to cross the 20-seat mark, something that is not frequently seen elsewhere. The other aspect where loyalty comes to the fore is the state's regions attitude towards political parties—all regions in Maharashtra, from Vidarbha, Marathwada to western Maharashtra and Mumbai, have very predictable overall voting patterns. For instance, in Vidarbha, the Congress and the BJP have remained powerful forces; in Marathwada, the Shiv Sena and the BJP have been seeing big gains; western Maharashtra is the NCP's bastion; whereas the Mumbai Metropolitan Region is the Shiv Sena's stronghold.

That most of these regions have been voting on similar lines for years now is a sign of just how loyal voters can be to political parties. Nothing exemplifies this loyalty more than this nugget: In 2014, all the four major political parties—the Shiv Sena, the BJP, Congress and the NCP—fought separately. Five years later, they fought in alliances—the Shiv Sena with the BJP, and the Congress with the NCP. But in both elections, the voting percentages of all the four parties remained nearly the same, with only minor variations in them. This means that voters remained loyal to the party—alliance or not.

If political loyalties are what define Maharashtra, in neighbouring Gujarat, a rather peculiar factor is the sharp divide in the proportion of rural and urban representation, electorally. Of the total 182 assembly seats in the state, only 42 are in the state's urban areas. The remaining, a whopping majority of 142 seats, are in the hinterlands.

In 2017, this disproportionate divide nearly changed the electoral fortunes of the ruling BJP. In the polls, the Congress won 71 seats in the rural areas, whereas the BJP could only manage to win 63 seats. The head start that the Congress got in the rural areas nearly won them the elections, but the BJP registered a thumping domination in the state's urban areas, winning 36 of the total 42 seats.[31] As a result, the final tally for both parties was close—the BJP won 99 seats, whereas the Congress and its allies won 81. If either of the two parties had dominated the rural areas, they would have easily emerged the winner.

But eastern India—the politically important states being Odisha, Bihar, Jharkhand, Chhattisgarh and West Bengal—offers a contrast in terms of economic prosperity and education levels. Both values for these states are low as compared to the West and the South. Besides, they have a significant tribal population that adds to the low indices of education and economic levels. The interesting thing is that while in the West, economic prosperity leads to political stability, in the East, the relative lack of educational and economic levels does the same! People here are more dependent on their political rulers—the *mai-baap*—and trust them to deliver them from the plight they find themselves in. They are in dire need of support from the political system, which is why they are loathe to make too many frequent changes. Perhaps, they also believe that one party is as good (or as bad) as another, and there is really no point in frequent changes in governments.

Given their socio-economic plight, the people are happy enough if they get something, anything, by way of relief. Not only are they happy but they feel indebted to the party that offers them even symbolic support. Things like food grain for the poorest free of cost (even if the product is barely fit for

[31]PTI, 'Urban Voters Still With BJP, Rural Gujarat Behind Congress', *NDTV*, 20 December 2017, https://bit.ly/3HZr91h. Accessed on 6 December 2023.

human consumption) or some sort of healthcare centre (even if the doctors are generally away and the supplementary staff is ill-equipped) are lapped up by way of 'progress'.

There is yet another phenomenon. Voters from the eastern states love leaders who are (or at least appear to be) down-to-earth, not too sophisticated (the more rustic the better) and live the life of a commoner. Thus, a Lalu Prasad Yadav could rule for years at a stretch despite being a poor administrator, and one who was enveloped in controversies and scandals. Ditto for Mamata Banerjee. On the other hand, Jyoti Basu (Bengal) and Manik Sarkar (Tripura) had spotlessly clean images, being also seen as 'commoners'; the voters reposed their trust in them for decades in one go.

Historically common tradition has it that the Northeastern regional parties—especially those in government—have to align with whoever is in power in New Delhi because of its dependency for Centre funds, but this approach is slowly changing. Emergence of strong leaders like the BJP's Hemanta Biswa Sarma and Meghalaya Chief Minister Conrad Sangma are accelerating this change. The Modi government also understands that the Northeast contributes 25 Lok Sabha seats, and emphasis has been given to infrastructure development.

Finally, the North. This is arguably the most tricky and fascinating part of geography and demography in terms of elections. The literacy level, here, is relatively low, the educational infrastructure is far from satisfactory and the health infrastructure is creaky. For decades, states of North India have been categorized informally as 'sick' or '*bimaru*' in many respects. While things have been changing for the better in recent years, there is a lot that still needs to be done for the North to catch up with the rest.

The situation could have resulted in two kinds of responses from the voters. One, resignation to their fate, and two, an unusual belligerence that channelizes its fury during elections, voting out governments mercilessly and routinely. In Uttar Pradesh, Rajasthan, Madhya Pradesh and Haryana, state governments have lasted generally for not more than two successive terms. The people have low levels of trust when it comes to their political rulers. In fact, political parties themselves have low levels of trust with one another, even when they come together. Think of the various alliances that Uttar Pradesh has had in the last few decades and how they have all failed—from the Congress–SP, the SP–BSP and even the BSP–BJP. In Haryana, too, various political coalitions were struck and undone. When political leaders are not loyal to their allies, one shouldn't expect much from the voters!

There is something in the soil of North India that makes voters aggressive; perhaps the history of kings and rulers, of conquests and of pride, even when everything they value is stripped from them... They are difficult to satisfy, unlike their eastern counterparts. It is perhaps the 'ego' that is at work—both in the leaders and the voters.

~

8

WOMEN AS A SWING FACTOR

'I've learned that people will forget what you said, people will forget what you did, but people will never forget how you made them feel.'

—Maya Angelou

Since the beginning of civilization, women have kept households running by making prudent choices between needs and wants. In twenty-first-century India, their increasing participation in the workforce and in independent decision-making due to financial self-sufficiency and women's liberation, have led to a marked rise in women exercising their franchise—from 53.3 per cent women voter turnout in 2004[32] to 67.2 per cent in 2019[33]. Political parties have been quick to take note

---

[32]Press Information Bureau, 'General Elections 2014: Highest Ever Voter Turn-Out', Election Commission, Government of India, 21 May 2014, https://bit.ly/3xkvOWt. Accessed on 14 February 2023.

[33]Jain, Bharti, 'Women Voter Participation Exceeds That of Men in 2019 LS Polls: CEC Chandra', *The Times of India*, 26 November 2021, https://bit.ly/3K1XDul. Accessed on 14 February 2023.

of the change and recalibrate their political strategy.

In addition to minority appeasement, pro-poor politics and caste politics, politicians are discovering a brand new vote bank that is helping them sail through elections—the female voter. My reading of the several state and national elections over the past decade is that there is an unmistakable emerging trend—the unshakeable leaders almost always enjoy the overwhelming support of women voters. Be it Prime Minister Narendra Modi or chief ministers M.G. Ramachandran, Arvind Kejriwal, Naveen Patnaik or J. Jayalalithaa, they have especially watched out for women voters and received appreciation and votes in reciprocation. Bihar Chief Minister Nitish Kumar too appealed to this vote bank and caught the popular imagination by his 'Sushasan Babu' image. The prohibition of alcohol under his last regime and the distribution of cycles to girl students have been hugely popular with the women electorate.

While standard operating procedures and schemes for women have taken up a key section in the election manifestos that are now distinctly segmented keeping in mind the target audiences, leaders tirelessly pander to the '*mataon, behnon aur betiyon*' (mothers, sisters and daughters) of the nation, knowing full well that women hold the key to their fortunes.

Modi's second term in office is largely thanks to the delivery of promises made in 2014. There were three very successful schemes that proved to be a game changer in 2019—free gas connections (Ujjwala), toilets (Swachh Bharat) and housing for all (Pradhan Mantri Awas Yojana)—and all of them had the woman voter at the centre of their marketing strategy. Modi talked of giving women the luxury of smokeless kitchens and the dignity of a private toilet, and pandered to the *grihalakshmi* in them through his pet projects.

All that Modi had to do was rename the Indira Awas Yojana, deliver it right and publicize it well among his target audience, and he had the perfect formula to win hearts. These have remained the central theme of his rallies since he came to power in 2014, and my surveys ahead of the 2019 general elections clearly indicate that the resounding mandate he got was based largely on the backing of women voters. The Modi government's audacious legislation, criminalizing triple talaq following the Supreme Court's verdict abolishing the regressive practice, was yet another move to woo women from a community that has traditionally been wary of the BJP.

Delhi Chief Minister Arvind Kejriwal, who won his third consecutive election in 2020, offered a slew of freebies targeted at women. He introduced free bus and metro rides for women and spoke of ways to ramp up women's security through better street lights, CCTV cameras and marshals in public buses. The makeover of government schools with parent–teacher meetings, summer camps, English-speaking classes and swanky campuses left mothers highly impressed, while free water and power made him their messiah.

Kejriwal had zeroed in on his audience well in advance and through his campaign, referred to himself as '*aapka bada bhai* (your elder brother)' or '*ghar ka bada beta* (the elder son of your family)'. For a government to come back with such a clean sweep is a clear verdict of its popularity, and this happened because women threw their weight behind him.

Unlike minority or caste-based voting patterns, there is no homogeneity in the voting trends of women. It will be highly inaccurate if I were to say that women across the country went out to vote, making their own independent choices. But I will take the liberty of making another rather simplistic yet factual observation. If women voters were to be classified according to region, I would say women in the five southern states of Kerala, Tamil Nadu, Karnataka, Andhra Pradesh and Telangana vote independently (sans the influence of male members of the family), whereas in North India (if we were to consider the rest of the country) they go by the judgement of the dominant male in the household, usually the father, husband or father-in-law. Our interaction with women voters during surveys in a state like Rajasthan has been very limited. This is true for all of North India where the practice of purdah or *ghunghat* (veil) is prevalent—making them less accessible for seeking their opinion—compared to the South, where women are far more chatty and well-informed.

The link between literacy levels and financial independence with independent decision-making is undeniable. Literacy decides profession, which in turn decides a woman's financial status and independence of thought. If you are a working woman and contribute to the cumulative household income, your preferences begin to count and you become a part of the decision-making in the small and big issues at stake. This includes voting preferences.

As we all know, literacy rates in the southern states are way higher than in the rest of the country. This is true of the percentage of women in the active workforce too. But the nature of the job is not always as important as her financial independence. Literacy, however, means more informed choices and awareness of one's rights. I couldn't help but make this distinction between the voting patterns of women in South India and the rest of the country after it got me into serious trouble once. That is a story I am obligated to share, as it was one of the rare occasions we went wrong with my poll prediction—all because I ignored this important vote bank!

I wouldn't say we were lazy but that we extrapolated our experiences in the rest of the country, where men decide voting preferences for the entire family, to the voting patterns of women in Tamil Nadu. I am not making a casual, generic statement here, and I hope I won't draw the ire of the many strong, well-informed and educated women in the northern, eastern and western regions of the country. I am simply citing voting trends.

In these three regions, particularly in Rajasthan, Uttar Pradesh, Punjab, Haryana, Maharashtra, Gujarat, West Bengal and Odisha, our surveyors were told by women voters, primarily rural, that they would decide after speaking to the head of the family, who is always a male member. In most cases, they are too shy to even have a freewheeling conversation, and if they did confide in us and told us what they liked or disliked about a leader or the incumbent government, they mostly would not talk decisively of their choice of political party or candidate. Very often, they would say, '*Aap unse baat kar lijiye, woh jo kahenge*… (You speak to him, whatever he decides…).' We observed that whatever the men told us about their voting preference, the outcome or verdict was in line with it.

The Tamil Nadu story was an eye-opener of sorts and has been a major learning curve for me personally. In the summer of 2016, our surveyors fanned out across the state and were hard at work. It was a single-phase election, which meant less reaction time as we had to report exit polls the same day. Since the exit polls go on air by 6.30 p.m. as soon as voting concludes, we had to wrap up our survey by 4 p.m. and collate and crunch data as the clock ticked. We were using the archaic pen-and-paper technique during our survey, and due to paucity of time, we did not manage to cover female respondents in proportion to their voting percentage. Of course, the data collection took time because of the manual entry process, thus slowing us down further.

AMI predicted a win for DMK+, that is, the DMK-led coalition, with 124–140 seats out of the 232 seats on which polls were held (two seats were left out), with the AIADMK trailing at 89–101. The result, much to my chagrin, was just the opposite. The AIADMK won 135 seats while the DMK got 96. The margin of victory between the AIADMK and DMK–Congress was only 1.03 per cent, so it was a close contest, but I want to tell you exactly where we went wrong.

I took a hard look at our survey techniques before going back to the drawing board. In our exit poll, 88 per cent of the respondents were male and only 12 per cent were female. It was grossly skewed towards men; in our post-result analysis, we found that the female voters differed from the men in their choices. When we broke down the voting preferences shared with us in the survey, it was right there before us. Of the total male voters we surveyed, 36 per cent said they would vote for the AIADMK, 41 per cent chose the DMK, 10 per cent were for the Desiya Mupokku Dravida Kazhagam (DMDK) and the Congress and the BJP had 2 per cent each. Women openly backed Amma, J. Jayalalithaa. About 47 per cent women chose the AIADMK, 36 per cent went with the DMK, 8 per cent were for the DMDK, 2 per cent backed the BJP and 1 per cent were for the Congress. We were so close yet so far. While the responses were in line with the final results, our sample profile was all wrong. Not only did we switch to a more scientific data collection system through Computer-Assisted Personal

Interviews (CAPIs) on tablets for error-free and real-time data availability, we also started taking the opinion of women voters in this part of the country far more seriously.

Jayalalithaa held a special place in the hearts of women. Our surveyors later told me how women voters were staunch believers in Amma and were convinced that everything they owned, from home appliances to saris, were given to them by her. The men, however, felt a tad neglected and were hoping to bring 'Kalaignar', M. Karunanidhi, back to power. Evidently the women had their way.

To her supporters, Jayalalithaa, 'in spite of being a woman', was an authoritative personality. She had doled out household and kitchen appliances and utility products such as pressure cookers, gas stoves, fridges, television sets, utensils, saris and *shringar* kits. Even matchboxes and lighters were branded with her party symbol, the two leaves. She connected with the women in the state like no other did. Though Tamil Nadu did not see stable governments, Amma was larger than life. She was wise in having known the position of women in South Indian households and not neglecting this important vote base.

However, not all women leaders are seen as champions of the female electorate. West Bengal Chief Minister and TMC supremo Mamata Banerjee is popular for taking on the Left following years of misrule, while the BSP chief Mayawati is considered a Dalit mascot. None of them are seen as particularly indulgent towards women voters.

Our experience in the recent Bihar assembly polls was similar to Tamil Nadu in 2016. This time, though we did not repeat the mistake of neglecting the crucial female vote bank, we failed to make an accurate prediction since the exact voter turnout for male and female voters was not available until two days after the exit polls were announced. The overall female voter turnout was 5.13 per cent more than the male turnout, which was revealed to us much after the exit polls were aired. This female vote share was heavily in favour of the BJP–JD(U) alliance. In the first phase of voting, in which men marginally voted more than women with a difference of 2.47 per cent, our predictions were more or less in line with the results. We had predicted 50 seats for the MGB and they bagged 47, while we expected the BJP–JD(U) alliance to get 16 seats but it instead won 22. The second and third phases had a higher difference in the male and female voter turnouts—6.29 per cent and 10.64 per cent more women than men voted in the second and third phases respectively. Had these figures been announced earlier, our calculations might have been more accurate. To add to this, Covid-19 restrictions limited our number of women voter interviews. Unfortunately, this was the third time in my career as a psephologist that I was way off the mark.

In a marked difference from North Indian households, women in the South often confided in our surveyors and asked them not to tell the husband about their choice of party or candidate. We often came out of a house with two diametrically opposite views. In the North, that is unthinkable.

In my view, the rise in overall literacy rates in the country is inextricably linked to increase in voter turnout. From 59.9 per cent in 1999, we moved to 67.4 per cent in 2019 as educated and aware voters want to make every vote count. The literacy rate among women on a national average is 65.46 per cent as against 80 per cent among men, but the southern states fare much better than the North. According to Census 2011, literacy rates of women in Kerala (92.1 per cent), Tamil Nadu

(73.4 per cent) and Karnataka (68.1 per cent) are significantly higher than those in Uttar Pradesh (57.2 per cent), Madhya Pradesh (59.2 per cent), Rajasthan (52.1 per cent) and Bihar (51.5 per cent). Punjab (70.7 per cent) and Maharashtra (75.9 per cent) are exceptions here, but literacy rates are not directly proportional to women's workforce participation and, hence, cannot be the sole measure of their independence.

Cultural traditions and societal norms heavily dictate the position of women. Despite reasonably high rates of literacy, only 13.91 per cent women in Punjab are part of the combined rural and urban workforce; while in Kerala, it is just 18 per cent. In that respect, women in Andhra Pradesh (36.16 per cent), Karnataka (31.87 per cent) and Tamil Nadu (31.8 per cent) are better off in terms of their workforce participation.

While the female voter is being wooed like never before, political parties are yet to give them the importance they really deserve. The Women's Reservation Bill, proposing to grant 33 per cent reserved seats to women in the Lok Sabha and all state legislative assemblies, remains a distant dream. While women appeasement is all well and good, men in politics seem reluctant to share the space equally with women, rather like the erstwhile powerful royal families, where patriarchy was dominant.

The skewed contrast is global. How many women presidents can a superpower like the United States boast of? Telling, isn't it? Can men alone contribute to nation-building? Will that be a wholesome society? There is only one right answer to that. No!

~

9

INDIAN POOR VOTE MORE THAN THE RICH

The level to we invest ourselves in something is directly proportional to how much that investment is likely to give back to us. Politics is a patient witness to this give-and-take between political leaders and voters. Those who need or expect more from the leaders are more invested in realpolitik than those who have fewer expectations of or dependence on the government. This largely explains why rural India votes in such large numbers and why the upscale South Mumbai's voter turnouts are a national shame.

The underprivileged sections of society make sure that they vote for a party or candidate who will address their issues and take care of their needs. They exercise their voting rights because they are dependent on the government for their livelihood and general well-being, and the elected representatives are their first port of call when in distress. They reach out to the local leaders with a genuine expectation that their grievances will be addressed. The rich, however, are not dependent on the outcome of the government in a similar manner. They are more occupied with other pursuits related to work or leisure, and for them, voting is not a top priority. They vote only if it is convenient and in passing. In India, the definitions of poor and rich are as shocking as the disparity of wealth distribution.

Only around 6 per cent of the workforce in India files income tax returns. While the underprivileged across the country choose to vote diligently, the geography of the region too has a bearing on the voting pattern. A look at voting trends shows how the voter turnout percentage gradually falls as one moves from the rural areas to a small town to a major town and a metro. In the 2019 Assembly Elections in Maharashtra, Aheri, a rural constituency, recorded a voter turnout of 70.35 per cent, whereas in the posh locality Colaba, only 40 per cent of voters turned up to cast their ballot. In the 2018 Karnataka Assembly Elections, Tumkur Rural registered a voter turnout of 85.41 per cent, while the urban Bangalore South saw a low 52.86 per cent.

One reason for this difference is also that big cities have a large population of migrant workers who find it difficult to put their papers and documents together for want of a valid address or identity proof, without which they cannot vote. Political parties also find it easier to mobilize masses in rural areas, where people are more closely knit and generally more amenable to be brought together. When grassroots workers reach out to voters in one village or mohalla, they are able to mobilize the entire population in that area in one go.

This, however, is not possible in a city where residents live in gated colonies and apartments and live aloof, isolated lives—cut off from one another. In a village or small town, sometimes even when there are multiple elections in one go, say, when the assembly polls coincide with the gram, nagar or zila panchayat polls in which no election symbols are allotted, voters are fully aware of the candidates in the running in each of these elections, and they can easily identify them by their names. That is the level of awareness and interest that voters have in the electoral process in rural parts of the country. This is because, as mentioned earlier, their daily lives are tied to the outcome of these polls.

If we look at India as a whole, voter turnout is higher in the states where urbanization is relatively less. If we compare Madhya Pradesh and Maharashtra, we see a stark difference. Madhya Pradesh has a largely rural population, and in the absence of adequate private jobs, there is greater dependence on the rural economy. In the Assembly Elections of December 2018, the voter turnout was a whopping 74.61 per cent. Contrast this with Maharashtra's 2019 Assembly Elections, where the voter turnout was only 61.13 per cent.

In the General Elections of 2019, the all-India voter turnout stood at 67.11 per cent. As mentioned earlier, in India, 70 per cent voters are rural and the rest are urban. Of the 70 per cent, approximately 75 per cent go out to vote, which accounts for 52 per cent across India. In the urban areas, the average turnout is usually roughly 50 per cent, which makes it 15 per cent across India, adding up to 67 per cent approximately.

Tall leaders like Indira Gandhi and Narendra Modi read these trends and modelled their governance accordingly. Any leader who has addressed this section of the electorate has enjoyed long tenures—Jawaharlal Nehru, Jyoti Basu and Indira Gandhi, for example. In the 1990s, *India Today* conducted a survey on the best prime minister of India till then, and Nehru won hands down. He remained popular for generations after, and his winning streak can be credited to his pro-poor outlook.

Leaders such as Jyoti Basu, Naveen Patnaik, Manik Sarkar, M.G. Ramachandran, Raman Singh, Shivraj Singh Chouhan, J. Jayalalithaa and Narendra Modi were voted back to power as chief ministers because they addressed the concerns of the poor and never neglected this key vote bank. The MGNREGA was a clear-cut winner for Prime Minister Manmohan Singh when he introduced it in 2005.

While only the relatively rich pay income tax, the less rich also contribute to the exchequer through the goods and services tax (GST) and other indirect taxes. For any government, it is imperative to look after its people. However, not everyone is dependent on the government in a similar manner. The delivery of power, water and roads (*bijli*, *paani*, *sadak*) affects everyone. The rich use these amenities as much as the poor do. But public education, healthcare facilities and law and order touch only certain segments. The rich can afford expensive private schools and colleges or send their kids abroad. They can get the best medical treatment despite the costs involved and are free to hire their own security guards. The poor depend heavily on the government for good education, medical attention and a peaceful life.

We have often seen and read how the privileged get away even when they are on the wrong side of the law and the poor suffer even if they are not at fault. A strong government that fixes loopholes in the policing system and ensures a safe environment for its people has always been more popular with the poorer sections. However, for the poor, the first basic expectation is that the government of the day should provide livelihood support. The rich may prioritize anything—from pollution levels to the traffic situation, gardens and garbage collection, cleanliness, tax regime or the overall infrastructure—but the underprivileged seek the basics.

While the decisions of any government affect people uniformly, at times, it is like a see-saw. A move that works remarkably well for the poor does the very opposite for the privileged and vice versa. This analogy might not always work, but when it is at play, the government's job to strike a balance becomes even tougher. Modi's demonetization gambit is a big case in point.

Before talking about the impact of demonetization, let us rewind a bit and look at Modi and his takeover of the party at the national level. He was acutely aware of the BJP's baggage of 'pro-rich, pro-urban and pro-upper caste' image. Even today, political analysts will tell you how the party does remarkably better in urban pockets and big cities compared to the rural belts. When Modi took charge, he knew he had to shed that public perception if he was to govern sustainably and for long.

He knew the tried-and-tested strategy of the past was the key to governing India. However, the shift from pro-rich to pro-poor and pro-urban to pro-rural could not happen overnight. Modi began giving the BJP an image makeover by hard selling his own *chaiwala* days and reiterating his humble origins. While the setting of his birth was not the rustic village, he recreated the imagery of a young boy scurrying along a railway platform, handing out cups of the hot beverage to passengers. When he juxtaposed his days of hardship with the privileges of a dynast, he instantly connected with the masses, which let go the image of the BJP as being pro-rich. Modi held out the promise of looking after the poor mothers in the villages, not letting them suffer in the kitchen smoke, symbolic of their domestic drudgery. He promised dignity to women by building toilets. He sought 60 months, as opposed to the 60 years of Congress rule, and showcased Gujarat as the model of good governance.

After a thumping majority in the parliamentary polls of 2014, Modi seemed to be on a winning spree, winning Maharashtra, Jharkhand and Haryana that year. I would, however, attribute those victories to the 'revolving door' theory, as the states were simply itching for a change. In 2015, when the United States President Barack Obama visited India, Modi was sucked into a controversy with his fancy hologram suit and Maybach glasses. The opposition made hay while the sun shone on them through the following months. Modi's popularity took a hit for the first time and the consequent losses in Delhi and Bihar polls made it worse. Despite Lalu Prasad Yadav's corrupt image, his alliance with Nitish Kumar sailed through. Kejriwal wooed the common man, while Modi yet again fell into the perception trap and the states went to opposition parties one after the other. Even as Modi rolled out his pro-poor schemes like the Jan Dhan Yojana, the Ujjwala scheme and housing for all, the string of losses continued.

It was in this backdrop that, on 8 November 2016, Modi appeared before a national audience to announce what would be a huge game changer for him in the years to come. Modi's promise to bring back black money and deposit ₹15 lakh in every citizen's account had begun to be touted as a *jumla* (false promise). The promise was to check the circulation of black money and the said ₹15 lakh was just a metaphor. The mathematics was never that simple.

But in the face of mounting pressure, Modi decided to target the rich, the traders and black money holders, and overnight became the messiah of the poor. At the time, the note ban weakened the position of the business houses, traders and politicians; whereas for the poor, it might at best have been some sort of harassment to get their old notes exchanged for new currency notes. The poor live on daily wages and had few savings to lose. But even in those serpentine queues outside banks, the poor and the middle class rarely spoke against the note ban. When Modi admitted to the inconvenience and said that it was for the greater good of the honest taxpayer and the poor of the country, the people accepted it.

Interestingly, the timing of the demonetization was close to the Uttar Pradesh Assembly Elections slated for March 2017, in which incumbent Chief Minister Akhilesh Yadav had begun to come across as a strong contender despite many accusations against him. The note ban was probably an image correction effort as much as it was to convey to the people that Modi had always been serious about bringing back black money. The move worried those who had stacks of cash, but the underprivileged stood on the fringes gleefully watching the plight of the haves. What worked like a dream in this gambit was how money started flowing into the accounts of the poor as the black money hoarders tried to save their cash by diverting it into the accounts of their domestic help and other staff.

Even as the poor were told that this money would have to be eventually returned and that it did not belong to them, the joy of seeing one's account swell is indescribable. The poor are a victim of the arrogance of the rich, but with the latter now turning to them for desperate help, it tipped the uneven scales in favour of the poor. While it was beyond their expectations that their accounts would have lakhs of rupees, the thrill of seeing the employer or the local heavyweight beseeching them was overwhelming; once the money goes into someone else's account, you cannot even mistreat them. I have heard several first-hand experiences to say this with certainty that a large number of people who rescued their richer acquaintances, employers, friends, felt that 'if not ₹15 lakh, at least something has come into my account', and that Modi finally did it. Interestingly, given the huge groundswell of support among the masses for the decision, even large sections of corporate India, or the rich, were compelled to hail demonetization.

We did a survey before the Uttar Pradesh elections on whether demonetization was a good idea. We found a clear indication that people had voted in its favour. Around 57 per cent of the respondents said it was a good decision, 30 per cent said it was a bad decision, 11 per cent said it had no impact and 2 per cent remained undecided. The BJP won the 2017 election handsomely, dashing the hopes of its rivals that demonetization would swing the votes in their favour.

Demonetization worked like a dream for Modi. I would say that even the 2019 parliamentary polls victory can be partially attributed to the image makeover—from pro-rich to pro-poor—that Modi and his party affected.

~

10

THE POLITICS OF CASTE

The story of democratic India's electoral politics would be incomplete without an understanding of caste as an essential component of victories and defeats. All political parties, without exception, use caste arithmetic to plot their election strategies, whether it is a Lok Sabha election or state assembly polls. So much so that over the decades, parties with a dedicated caste base have emerged. They have openly flaunted caste credentials to gain votes, and have been pretty successful, even if only at the state level. The caste factor often becomes a key, if not always the central, determinant in the formation of a cohesive bond between the three pivots of electoral politics that we began this book with—voters, leaders and governance.

The number of castes and sub-castes in the country is baffling, making it even more of a challenge for any political party to win them over. Each has their own aspirations and needs, but they all are united in the desire for greater empowerment and stakeholding in the country's political system. There are as many as 3,000 castes and some 25,000 sub-castes in the country.

The problem with the caste system was (and by many

accounts, still is) that it puts the underprivileged sections of the society, especially the Shudras—called the Oppressed Classes and later the SCs—to an enormous disadvantage. Traditionally, they were the least educated, at times uneducated, and this meant that the doors of empowerment were shut to them. They could not get good jobs and so were financially weak. They were considered the lowermost in the caste hierarchy—outcastes—and thereby socially shunned by the upper castes.

The issue of governance had been settled with the old varna system in place. But with independence and the ushering of electoral democracy in 1952, the Indian social environment witnessed a massive churning. Even before, leaders such as B.R. Ambedkar and Mahatma Gandhi had taken up cudgels on behalf of the SCs, demanding an end to discrimination—though the methods were so different that it often resulted in clash of ideas between the two leaders. While Ambedkar attacked Hinduism itself for the prevalent caste discrimination and demanded its drastic overhaul, Gandhi believed that a social change alone could rid the nation of the evil. The change had to come from within, he argued, through persuasion and not confrontation. One of the methods he employed was calling the SCs Harijans or the men of God. Steeped in religious thoughts, he felt that associating the SCs with God would strike a chord with the people; it was an old social tactic to invoke God to get ordinary mortals to do the right thing.

There were others, such as Acharya Vinoba Bhave, Jyotiba Phule and Erode Venkatappa Ramasamy 'Periyar', who, in their own different ways, contributed to the fight against caste discrimination. Periyar founded the Dravidian movement in what is today's Tamil Nadu, and the two main Dravida parties, the DMK and the AIADMK, have flourished over the decades, building upon the foundation that Periyar laid down.

Whatever the solutions, it became clear that the old order could no longer sustain. Still, the mindset of caste discrimination continued right until the 1990s. The privileged sections held that if the SCs were granted empowerment, they would become too bold and refuse to do their bidding, in both political and social terms. For instance, there was no surety that they would follow instructions on whom to vote for, or that they would do the menial tasks they were traditionally engaged in.

The problem was: How could the SCs, not being equipped with either education or skills, hope to compete with the rest, who had the advantage, passed on through generations, of both education and skills? The concept of positive discrimination through reservations in education and government jobs thus came about.

The role of the SCs in electoral outcomes would now come into play. In 1952, for the first time, independent India had an elected government. Those who entered Parliament became the 'representatives of the people'. A carpenter's son no longer confined his dreams and aspirations to being a carpenter. Instead, he began to think: If I can contribute in the formation of a government, I can also hope to represent the government someday. The power of electoral democracy became the turning point. Cabinets were formed keeping in mind various caste representations, tickets were distributed keeping caste equations in consideration.

Political leaders, quick to realize the gains in winning over the confidence of the underprivileged in terms of caste, also factored in minority religious groups, especially the Muslims, since they too suffered from many of the problems associated with the SCs. For leaders, Muslims were low-hanging fruits. They were educationally and socially backward, but they additionally suffered from a sense of insecurity that had come from the horrors of Partition. Therefore, the SCs and the Muslims were seen by political leaders as a target audience around which a long-term vote bank could be constructed.

The reasoning was simple: You can only feed the hungry. You can only fill a glass that is empty. Politicians were quick to realize the electoral potential in cultivating the SCs, who had the most needs and grievances. It was but natural that the Congress party and its leaders were the prime beneficiaries of the approach because the Congress was the only dominant party, nationally as well as in the states, for decades since Independence. That domination, at least nationally, would continue through till the 1984 Lok Sabha elections.

On coming to power, Indira Gandhi realized the true potential of tapping into the SC vote. Before her, neither Jawaharlal Nehru nor Lal Bahadur Shastri felt the need to treat them as vote banks, as their other credentials were enough to keep them afloat. Who the leader is rarely matters to the privileged or well-to-do people; whoever the leader or the party in power may be, they can manoeuvre their way to gains. But the deprived sections of society rely almost entirely on the leadership, their mai-baap, for relief. Indira Gandhi was prompt in understanding this, and thus her politics revolved around popular slogans (*Garibi hatao*) and measures that claimed to better the lives of millions of the under-privileged.

The decision of the V.P. Singh government to implement the recommendations of the Mandal Commission to give reservation to OBCs dramatically changed caste politics across the country. Now, V.P. Singh donned the mantle of the messiah of the backward classes—essentially a grouping of various castes and sub-castes, barring the SCs and STs. Mandal politics also gave rise to a new set of leaders who would, in their respective states, form their own political outfits hinged on the support of a particular caste affiliation.

Mulayam Singh Yadav formed the SP and Kanshi Ram founded the BSP in Uttar Pradesh. In neighbouring Bihar, another Mandal leader, Lalu Prasad Yadav, established the RJD. Both Lalu and Mulayam made no bones of the fact that their parties depended on the overwhelming support of the Yadavs—a party of the Yadavs, by the Yadavs and for the Yadavs. Similarly, Kanshi Ram (and later his mentee Mayawati) latched on the backing of the SCs.

Incidentally, all these three parties initially tried to incorporate the OBCs into its fold but later concentrated on their core caste strengths. They also wooed the upper castes, but succeeded only when the upper castes had no option but to support them. For example, in the 2002 Uttar Pradesh Assembly Elections, the SP got sizeable support from the upper castes because neither the Congress nor the BJP were strong in the state. In 2007, the upper castes switched their support to Mayawati. Neither the SP nor the BSP was their preferred choice; it was a choice out of having no option.

In more recent years, however, an unlikely party has managed to appropriate for itself the gains of Mandal politics: the BJP. During V.P. Singh's reign, it had countered Mandal politics with its temple movement and was largely seen as a pro-upper caste party. However, with Narendra Modi occupying centre stage since 2014, the party has managed to win over a large number of the OBCs, with few exceptions such as the Yadavs. But even here, it does throw some surprises off and on—its recent victory in the Azamgarh Lok Sabha by-poll, despite the presence of a large Yadav vote base, is a case in point. As an aside, the BJP also managed to win from Rampur in the Lok Sabha by-election despite the presence of sizeable Muslim voters and the influence of the SP's strongman, Azam Khan.

A similar disruption has been evident in the case of Mayawati's BSP. Over the last few years, the BJP has chipped away at her vote bank, winning over the non-Jatav sub-caste. The outcome has been disastrous for Mayawati; her party drew a blank in the 2019 Lok Sabha elections and fared miserably in the 2017 and the 2022 Assembly Elections in Uttar Pradesh.

The contours of caste politics have undergone a major shift during the last decade, with conventional mathematics falling by the wayside. When Mayawati and Akhilesh Yadav came together to confront the BJP in elections, it seemed like an unbeatable combination—the Yadavs and the SCs, together with the Muslims. Again, when the SP and the Congress party joined hands, it seemed that the BJP would lose out. But in both the cases, the combination failed. This was primarily due to the decisive shift of the non-Jatav votes towards the BJP in the first case and the near complete consolidation of non-Yadav votes in BJP's favour for the latter.

In the 2022 Assembly Elections, Mayawati's party secured just one seat out of 403, the Congress got two while 111 seats went to the SP; the BJP ended up with 273 seats as a result of the massive reverse consolidation towards it. A more or less similar trend was evident in the 2019 Lok Sabha elections. Although the SP and the BSP fought the polls together, the magic did not work for the same two reasons that were seen later in 2022. The non-Jatav voted en bloc for the BJP, thus reducing the BSP's leverage, and the OBCs, minus the Yadavs, also backed the BJP, thus cancelling out the BSP–SP combined strength of Yadav, Muslim and Jatav votes. The same had been the case in Madhya Pradesh in the 2019 elections, where the Jatav sub-caste supported the Congress party but the non-Jatav votes went to the BJP. With the division in SC votes, and its own consolidation of upper caste and OBC votes, the BJP romped home.

But, while the results of Uttar Pradesh (and Bihar) elections are usually cited to show the BJP's prowess in managing caste votes, it is actually in Karnataka that the party did a miraculous job. In the 2019 General Elections, the party won 25 of the 28 seats. One was won by an independent supported by the BJP. The Congress and the JD(S) were left with just one seat each. The JD(S) was defeated in nearly all of its strongholds, including Mandya despite boasting of the support of its core voters, the Vokkaliga community. Congress stalwart Mallikarjun Kharge also lost. Here too, the non-Jatav votes went to the BJP, along with its traditional votes of the Lingayat community, leaving its rivals stranded.

Caste equations decide elections elsewhere too. For instance, in Haryana, Jat politics has been dominant, with several Jat leaders—Devi Lal and his family being among the most prominent—managing or influencing the political fortunes of the state. With the tag of being an upper-caste party, or at least a strong leaning towards the upper castes, and with a history of not been enthusiastic about the implantation of the Mandal Commission's recommendations, the BJP had a difficult task ahead. It could not hope to win in many states, let alone nationally, on its own strength, without gaining the confidence of the SCs and the OBCs. Enter Narendra Modi in 2014.

Modi had already acquired a brand image as chief minister

of Gujarat, from the end of 2001 right until 2013, after which he came on the national stage. The so-called Gujarat Model was touted as the showpiece of his administrative and governance skills. But it was his 'other' image—that of a man who had seen poverty from close quarters, that worked in his favour at the national level.

Modi also had to contend with the image of the Rashtriya Swayamsevak Sangh (RSS), the umbrella organization to which the BJP belonged. He had served in the RSS for decades before entering politics as Gujarat's chief minister. The RSS had been founded in 1925 as a counter to the growing influence of Muslim politics and the perceived sidelining of the aspirations of Hindus. Naturally, the RSS was seen as pro-Hindu (and by extension, anti-Muslim). Besides, the RSS was seen as a social organization that was managed by the well-off and the upper castes, especially the Brahmins. While this image had served the RSS well in the initial decades of its founding, the changed social, political and economic conditions in the country over the years required a remake of that image. Modi had to handle that aspect as well.

He leveraged his own life story to project the message of the BJP being inclusive, with its appeal not limited to urban voters and upper castes. He reminded the people in his 2014 election campaign at rally after public rally that he had risen from the bottom, and that he had served tea at a small railway station in his hometown. His managers also consistently put across the message that Modi himself belonged to the OBC, that he understood their needs and aspirations and that he was best placed to fulfil them. His well-recorded competence as an administrator came in handy to convince the voters that he could do what he was promising.

Over the years, as results have demonstrated and as mentioned earlier, the BJP, under Modi's leadership, has managed to win over large sections of the OBC votes as well those of the SCs. This did not happen by accident but was the outcome of a well-planned strategy in image makeover. It would not be wrong to say that the brand 'Modi' evolved with time, all the while bringing electoral gains for his party, even as his rivals struggled to find ways to stop the migration of their vote banks.

The BJP, under Modi, also cracked another vote bank, the STs, which traditionally voted for the Congress party despite the emergence of several regional parties across the country. In the 2014 Lok Sabha elections, the BJP beat the Congress. While the BJP's vote share rose by 14 per cent, that of the Congress declined by 10 per cent. As stated in *The Hindu*,

> The Congress's performance was no better in constituencies that were reserved for the STs. It won only 3 ST reserved constituencies in this election compared to the 2009 Lok Sabha election, where it won in 20 ST reserved constituencies. On the other hand, the BJP secured 24 seats, an increase of 14 seats from the 2009 Lok Sabha election. The States where the nature of the contestation is mainly bi-polar, i.e., the Congress and BJP are in straight contest (Chhattisgarh, Gujarat, Maharashtra, Madhya Pradesh and Rajasthan), the BJP has won all seats in the ST reserved constituencies.[34]

[34]Mishra, Jyoti, 'Voting Patterns among Scheduled Tribes', *The Hindu*, 9 June 2014, https://bit.ly/3I2UAR7. Accessed on 6 February 2023.

Furthermore, it also stated,

> The post-poll data from seven States with moderate to high tribal populations reveals that in four of them the BJP outperformed the Congress in terms of tribal support. These are Rajasthan, Maharashtra, Madhya Pradesh and Jharkhand. In fact, the gains for the BJP in Maharashtra and Rajasthan among the ST community were massive. Whereas only two in ten STs had voted for the BJP in Rajasthan in 2009, the figure this time jumped to six in ten. Meanwhile in Gujarat where the Congress had a huge lead over the BJP among tribals in 2009, the battle between the two parties for the tribal votes was very close. In Odisha, it was the Biju Janata Dal (BJD) which led the Congress among the tribal voters with the BJP in third place. Only Chhattisgarh—with a tribal population of 31 per cent—saw the Congress making gains compared to the previous election, but here too the contest with the BJP was close.[35]

India's tribes also have their leaders whose activism resulted in not just a greater awareness of tribal communities of the country but also nudged the political leadership into acknowledging their grievances, needs, aspirations and demands. The mainstreaming of STs into the larger society as well as into the political sphere too gained ground as a consequence of the heightened awareness. Some of these leaders played a stellar role in the fight for independence, while others dedicated themselves to the upliftment of the tribal communities thereafter. The support of the STs has become an

---

[35]Ibid.

important element in electoral politics. While there have been many tribal leaders, the name of Birsa Munda (from present-day Jharkhand) comes readily to mind. He was a revolutionary and worked to reform his community and make it mainstream; in the process, he gained such a stature that his supporters referred to him as 'bhagwan'.

We can end this chapter with an interesting trivia. The Lok Sabha constituency of Valsad is unique. Since the 1952 General Elections, the party whose candidate has won from here is also the party that gave the country its prime minister post that election!

VALSAD LOK SABHA DETAILS—1957 ONWARDS

YEAR	WINNER	WINNER PARTY	PM NAME AND PARTY
1957	Nanubhai Patel	INC	Jawaharlal Nehru (INC)
1962	Nanubhai Patel	INC	Jawaharlal Nehru (INC)
1967	Nanubhai Patel	INC	Indira Gandhi (INC)
1971	Nanubhai Patel	INC (O)	Indira Gandhi (INC)
1977	Nanubhai Patel	JP	Morarji Desai (JP)
1980	Uttambhai Patel	INC (I)	Indira Gandhi (INC)
1984	Uttambhai Patel	INC	Rajiv Gandhi (INC)
1989	Arjunbhai Patel	JD	Vishwanath Pratap Singh (JD)
1991	Uttambhai Patel	INC	P.V. Narasimha Rao (INC (I))
1996	Manibhai Chaudhary	BJP	Atal Bihari Vajpayee (BJP)

1998	Manibhai Chaudhary	BJP	Atal Bihari Vajpayee (BJP)
1999	Manibhai Chaudhary	BJP	Atal Bihari Vajpayee (BJP)
2004	Kishanbhai Vestabhai Patel	INC	Manmohan Singh (INC)
2009	Kishanbhai Vestabhai Patel	INC	Manmohan Singh (INC)
2014	K.C. Patel	BJP	Narendra Modi (BJP)
2019	K.C. Patel	BJP	Narendra Modi (BJP)

11

SUCCESS MANTRA: TWO CASE STUDIES

When the appropriate stars for a person are in complete alignment, as they say in astrology, nothing adverse can happen to him. Even if setbacks happen, they can be overcome sooner than later with corrective prescriptions. In India's electoral democracy, its pivots are the stars: leaders, voters and governance. As long as there is lasting cohesion among them, a continuing alignment, leaders and political parties taste victory after victory. Even the factor of anti-incumbency fails to dent the prospect of winning.

Two states offer a perfect example of this phenomenon, one in the East and other in the West: Odisha and Gujarat. In the first case, the same leader and the same political party has been at the helm since 1999, braving many challenges and controversies. In the second, the same party has been dominant since 1995, getting the mandate to rule for the seventh straight term in 2022. Barring this commonality, the two states cannot be more different from each other. Gujarat is an industrial powerhouse, and it has a robust agricultural sector as well. In comparison, Odisha is a poor state, though rich in natural resources. While there has been considerable economic progress in the decades of Naveen Patnaik's rule, the state lags in many social indicators.

Given this divergence, the voters have had different expectations from their political leaders and governments. While in Gujarat, the political rulers are expected to address the need for an even greater economic and agricultural progress—a scaling up of the so-called Gujarat Model that gained popularity during Narendra Modi's three terms as chief minister—the masses in Odisha seek better housing, job opportunities, greater access to quality healthcare, better connectivity in terms of roads and other infrastructure.

Despite the emerging as well as old challenges, both the Biju Janata Dal (BJD) in Odisha and the BJP in Gujarat have repeatedly returned to power. Regardless of the lament of their critics or of the occasional shortfalls in governance, the voters have reposed trust in the leaders of the two parties in the respective states. They must be doing something right to retain the confidence of the people. That 'right' is what this chapter began with—a near-perfect alignment of voters, leaders and governance.

Odisha

Naveen Patnaik became the chief minister of Odisha for the first time in 1999. He came with the baggage of dynasty, being the son of the popular state leader Biju Patnaik, in whose name he founded the regional party, the BJD, in 1997. He started off with several disadvantages. One, being Biju Patnaik's son, he faced relentless media attention and speculation on whether he would fit into his father's shoes. Two, he had no experience of governance; indeed, his understanding of the state was far from comprehensive, and he had trouble even communicating with the people in the local language. Three, the state's economy was precarious. And four, he assumed charge in the aftermath of a massive cyclone that had devastated coastal Odisha, and the onerous task of relief and rehabilitation stared in his face.

Naveen Patnaik realized that the sooner he came out of his father's shadow, the better it would be for his political future. Therefore, unlike the other dynast leaders in the country, he did not go overboard in flaunting his family credentials. Instead, he busied himself in understanding the nitty-gritty of governance. Given the prevalent economic and social conditions, he decided to substitute in place a welfarism model of governance. Plans, both short-term and long-term, were conceptualized and implemented. Bureaucrats soon learned that although new to governance, Naveen Patnaik had clarity of vision and understanding of how it should be translated into action on the ground.

An example of his proactive style, which fetched him nationwide recognition, was seen in his handling of the Kalahandi issue. Kalahandi had gained notoriety for starvation deaths. But today, starvation is history in this district. In January 2021, while inaugurating an irrigation project there, the Chief Minister pointed out that Kalahandi alone supplied as much rice as the combined quantity of 10 states to the central treasury. This became possible because of many food security programmes that his government launched successfully. He did not hesitate to take on additional financial burdens on the state by making rice available to the poor at low prices—over and above the subsidies that the union government provided.

In 2018, his government launched the state's own food security scheme, with benefits to reach a target group of 25 vulnerable populations. His resolve to eradicate hunger from Odisha not only brought him laurels but also ensured the loyalty of voters from all over the state, cutting across caste and religious barriers.

Farmers and women form a major chunk of voters in most states, and Odisha is no exception. No leader or party can hope to win elections without their backing. Naveen Patnaik's electoral strategy factored this critical element. He launched Mission Shakti in 2001, by which more than six lakh women self-help groups with over 70 lakh members were created. A separate directorate in the government was created to nurture this segment. The Krushak Assistance for Livelihood and Income Augmentation (KALIA) was launched to benefit small and marginal farmers, and a considerable sum of over ₹1,800 crore was earmarked for the purpose.

The alignment of voters, leaders and governance was taken to the grassroots, at the Panchayati Raj institutions, where he increased reservation for women to 50 per cent from 33 per cent during his father's time. For the 2019 Lok Sabha elections, his party reserved 33 per cent of the seats in the state for women.

Naveen Patnaik's willingness to take on financial liabilities in order to uplift the underprivileged would perhaps have landed the state's finances in trouble, but for the attention he gave to revenue generation. Right until the early 2000s, Odisha was among the most fiscally stressed states. In 2002–03, the debt to the state GDP ratio stood at over 50 per cent, when the national average was close to 34 per cent. The state government struggled to even disburse salaries to its employees.

But prudent fiscal management through rationalization of expenditure, agreements signed with the Centre and use of technology to streamline tax collections brought about a turnaround. Accepting the recommendations of the Twelfth Finance Commission, it enacted the Fiscal Responsibility and Budget Management Act in 2005 and amended it subsequently. Odisha became a revenue surplus state in 2005–06. In 1999–2000, the average cost of borrowing for the state was close to 13 per cent; it declined to less than seven per cent in 2020–21.

The Maoist threat had been one of the major obstacles in development. With the ramping up of road and other infrastructures, even regions such as Malkangiri, which were Red hotbeds, now have good roads and basic healthcare facilities. With law and order in place, the Maoist threat has receded considerably.

The cumulative result of Naveen Patnaik's success in bonding voters, leaders and governance has been that he and his party have been able to withstand electoral challenges—while the country was swept by Modi magic in 2014 and 2019, his BJD bucked the trend and held the fort; the same was the case in the assembly elections. The Chief Minister's personal charisma and the delivery of his governance has been such that even controversies regarding his government have failed to dent his image. He has been accused of being authoritarian and leaving governance to the bureaucrats. Mining and chit fund scams surfaced during his tenure. But Naveen Patnaik has weathered the storms, understanding the art and science of winning elections.

Gujarat

When Narendra Modi took over as the chief minister of Gujarat towards the end of 2021, he had a few things in common with Naveen Patnaik. Like Patnaik, he too was inexperienced in governance and administration; like Patnaik, he assumed charge in the aftermath of a natural disaster, the Bhuj earthquake; and, like Patnaik, he too would initially bank on the bureaucracy to feel his way around before establishing a grip on the administration.

His other challenges were very different, though. While the BJP was already in power before he arrived, with Keshubhai Patel as chief minister, the party and the government faced multiple criticism on account of poor administration, factionalism and laxity in relief and rehabilitation work in the wake of the earthquake. His proactive attitude in handling the immediate crises won him admirers, but there were more challenges round the corner. Barely months after taking charge, the Godhra train burning incident happened, followed by the communal riots in early 2002. While the situation was soon brought under control, many lives were lost. Modi was accused by his critics of indirectly, or even directly, aiding the rioters who targeted Muslim homes. It was a stigma that was to haunt him for years, and his opponents, even today, raise the matter dispite the Supreme Court clearing him of all charges.

Modi was a quick learner. Having had his trial by fire, he realized two things. One, there must never be another communal riot in the state during his tenure. Two, Gujarat needed a fresh model of governance that would be better than all previous governments' and, more importantly, bring the attention of the voters to development-based governance.

Industry needed a flip, agriculture needed a boost, irrigation schemes had to be revamped and extended and various sectors of infrastructure, from roads to electricity, needed a dose of urgency and quality.

Modi had one quality that Naveen Patnaik did not: He was an excellent orator and communicator. As chief minister, he would effortlessly connect with the masses, understand their grievances and address them. In the 2002 Assembly Elections, he led the BJP to a thumping win, and he would go on repeat victories in 2007 and 2012. While critics claimed that communal polarization had led to his win in 2002, which came on the heels of the riots, they had trouble explaining how the BJP, under his leadership, won the 2007 and 2012 elections as well. They failed to acknowledge that Modi's success in aligning the three pivots of leader, voter and governance, was the critical element in his continuing success, making him Gujarat's longest-serving chief minister.

As chief minister, Modi did not make the mistake of focussing on one sector but worked for holistic development. If he was seen as industry-friendly, he also brought about radical transformation in the agriculture sector. He used technology in governance, which contributed to a check on corruption as also speedy delivery of welfare schemes. The Vibrant Gujarat Global Summits, during his tenure, attracted global attention, besides being attended by the who's who of the Indian industry. Investments poured in. 'More governance and less government' was a theme he adopted as chief minister.

While a lot has been said about his pro-industry policies in Gujarat, as chief minister, he initiated a massive programme with the help of NGOs and self-help communities, for the creation of groundwater conservation projects. By December

2008, more than 113,000 check dams had been constructed, which helped improve the groundwater levels.[36] The introduction of genetically modified cotton cultivation resulted in a boom in the state's agricultural sector, which grew at an average of more than 9 per cent from 2001 to 2007.[37]

If urban Gujarat flourished during his tenure as chief minister, rural Gujarat wasn't left behind either. With electricity reaching every village, the lives of millions of people underwent a dramatic change. Farmers were happy, and so were the others. One of the innovative measures was the Jyotigram Yojana, under which the supply of agricultural electricity was separated from the other rural electricity supply, thus ensuring better quality of power supply.

Later on, in his bid for prime ministership, Modi would invoke the Gujarat Model of development, and it clicked with the people. It did not happen because of smart messaging and PR, as his critics would like to believe. The Model talk worked because people in Gujarat had not only seen but experienced development, both at the urban and the rural levels. This is not to say that his governance as chief minister was flawless; indeed, there were reports that the scale of achievements was not what was being projected. But, as in the case of Naveen Patnaik, the voters were willing to overlook or forgive Modi's slip-ups because of his overall success in meeting their needs, aspirations and demands.

---

[36]'Gujarat Government Releases Check Dam Figures', *The Times of India*, 16 June 2016, https://bit.ly/3ZatXj6. Accessed on 24 February 2023.

[37]ET Bureau, 'Gujarat Records Highest Decadal Agricultural Growth Rate of 10.97%', *The Economic Times*, 16 July 2011, https://bit.ly/3y88TOJ. Accessed on 24 February 2023.

12

ELECTION RESULTS AND TECHNOLOGY

Indian elections have evolved a lot like Indian arranged marriages. Family or village elders, puffing on the communal hookah, no longer seal the fate of a candidate. Technology has left the ubiquitous *nai* (barber), who traditionally brought leads for probable matches and had a high success rate, redundant. How many parents, worried sick over their ward's insouciance, now ask their barber to find them a match or run a quick background check? Hardly any. Social media snooping is for millennials. Be it to shortlist potential alliances on a matrimonial site or to zero down on a local representative, a comparative analysis today is just a click away.

Similarly, technology has enabled voters today to share notes and build a consensus on who is 'deserving'. Earlier, the lack of communication channels kept them clueless about the views of voters in other parts of the country. Hence, decision-making largely remained localized, limited to a village, town, district or, at most, a state. The elderly, the socially empowered or the dominant caste/community could loosely be called 'influencers' back then, be it in an arranged marriage or an election.

Till the early 1990s, during polls, we could interact only with our immediate neighbourhood—even landline phones were then a luxury. Our physical reach limited our discussions and deliberations over whom to vote for, who was a deserving candidate, the government's performance, anti-incumbency and the like. Through tea shops and *nai-dukaan adda*s (corner shops, barber shops), social gatherings and lunch breaks at the workplace, opinions travelled merely by word of mouth.

The arrival of smartphones and social media has collapsed all physical boundaries and instantly connected everyone at a national and global level. In 2019, India had 373.88 million smartphone users, a sharp hike from 2017, when this figure stood at 299.24 million. According to a Comscore report, YouTube had 325 million unique monthly users in India as of May 2020. In 2021, according to then Union Minister for Communications, Electronics and Information Technology and Law and Justice Ravi Shankar Prasad, India has over 530 million WhatsApp users, over 400 million Facebook users, and over 10 million Twitter users—all essential campaign platforms for political parties.

Voters have always wanted a strong government. I see it like selecting the head of a family or a company. Unlike the olden times, the seniormost or eldest is now no longer the first choice. Instead, one looks for a strong and deserving successor to sort out the myriad challenges that the post-modern world has thrown up. Of course, the definition of 'deserving' is entirely relative, and I am not getting into that.

On social media, ideas crystallize and trend, leading to uniform opinions being formed and thumping majorities for the winner and, conversely, absolute negation of the loser. Whether it is positive or negative publicity, it gets communicated across the board. Opinions are shaped not only by trending ideas and raging debates on social media but also by ground realities reported from across the country. Social media has truly become a melting pot where opinions are formed in an unorganized and spontaneous manner and quite effortlessly. Thanks to the platform, it has nudged, or rather awakened, the citizen journalist in each of us. Of course, some opinions are carefully crafted by political parties, which will be addressed shortly.

The 2014 Lok Sabha elections, the Assembly Elections in Delhi and Bihar in 2015, Kerala and West Bengal in 2016 and Uttar Pradesh in 2017, all gave clear, resounding majorities to a single party or an alliance. In Delhi, Arvind Kejriwal's AAP wiped out the opposition by grabbing 67 out of 70 seats in February 2015, just 13 months after Delhi threw up a hung Parliament. From bagging 28 seats in his electoral debut in December 2013 and a 49-day stint as chief minister, Kejriwal came back as a giant in early 2015, as consensus built over the months that he could deliver if he had the numbers. This was barely eight months after the BJP swept all seven parliamentary seats in Delhi in the 2014 General Elections. The same was repeated in the 2019 parliamentary polls and the 2020 Delhi Assembly Elections, where again the BJP and AAP swept the state respectively.

Voters today make informed choices. They know which way the wind is blowing—the general pulse of the people is right out there. No one wants to waste their vote on the losing team. This explains why the Congress party, despite Sheila Dikshit's legacy, failed to better even its vote share in the Delhi polls. Instead, it dropped further from 9.7 per cent in 2015 to 4.2 per cent. Election after election, my interaction with voters during the pre- and post-poll surveys has convinced me that they know exactly what is on the table.

The AAP that was pushed to the third spot in Delhi with 18.11 per cent vote share in the 2019 Lok Sabha polls notched up to 53.57 per cent in the 2020 Assembly Elections, whereas the BJP that garnered 56.56 per cent in Delhi in the Lok Sabha polls managed to get only 38.51 per cent in the Assembly Elections. The staunchest Modi supporters clearly chose Kejriwal when it came to the local polls. This has been a nationwide trend. Who doesn't want to empower a solid leader? In Kerala, the LDF bagged 91 out of 140 seats. With 325 out of 403 seats in Uttar Pradesh, the BJP remained unshakeable. The two national elections of 2014 and 2019 are proof that Indian voters no longer want precarious, wobbly governments. No more rainbow coalitions. They want a strong leader and a solid majority that will push through definitive legislation.

The BJP has powered through a slew of pro-poor schemes like the Pradhan Mantri Ujjwala Yojana (free gas connection), Ayushman Bharat (health insurance worth ₹5 lakh), Pradhan Mantri Jan Dhan Yojana (zero balance bank account opening), soil testing for farmers, Swachh Bharat Mission and Mudra Yojana since 2014, which has lent Modi the image of an effective administrator. The fun part is that the political parties have been able to widen their reach manifold without their campaign budgets seeing a proportionate increase, thanks to cost-effective technological tools.

Back in the 1970s and 1980s, leaders, even the most hard-working of them, be it Indira Gandhi or Atal Bihari Vajpayee, could manage to pack in only a few rallies per day. Their audience remained only those they could reach and address physically. Leaders roughly managed five rallies or so a day even if they pushed themselves really hard at the hustings, and the next day, only a fraction of the population read about it in the newspapers. Today, every rally is telecast live on the social media handles of the respective political parties, instantly expanding the leader and the party's reach. Every speech recording is heard several times over and circulated through WhatsApp—long after it is delivered. In terms of physical reach too, multiple LED screens inside, and sometimes outside, the venue help pack in larger crowds at a single event. Sometimes, they are livestreamed across cities and towns, widening the targeted audience manifold.

Technology has thrown up interesting challenges for the Election Commission in the meantime. Political parties have found convenient ways to flout the model code of conduct that imposes restrictions on campaigning 48 hours before polling. Even as campaigning comes to a halt in a poll-bound state or constituency ahead of polling day, leaders move on to other constituencies, and the campaign continues live-streaming on everyone's smartphone. Technically, campaigning goes on till the last vote of the day is cast. Leaders usually get on with their campaigns in constituencies or states where there are no such restrictions, as elections are a few days or weeks away, killing two birds with one stone.

On a relaxed Sunday morning, 19 May 2019, as Prime Minister Narendra Modi sat meditating in a flowing saffron robe, with the snowclad Himalaya in the backdrop, his every move being live-streamed on news channels, voters across 59 constituencies trooped to polling booths to cast their votes. It was the seventh and final phase of voting, one that would be a direct verdict on Modi's governance. Large parts of key states like West Bengal, Madhya Pradesh, Uttar Pradesh, Punjab, Bihar and Himachal Pradesh were deciding whether Modi deserved another chance. All this—while the Prime Minister's brief detox at a 15-hour meditation session in a Kedarnath cave, which was termed as the first break in his five years of all-work-and-no-play stint—unfolded as a soft campaign that only advertising professionals can read into. Maybe others should take a page from such strategies because one is playing to win, after all. Though the Election Commission has laid down social media guidelines and is constantly working to plug all loopholes, politicians continue to get the better of it.

Effectively, communication has flowed in two directions—leader to voter and voter to voter—and both have led to an informal opinion formulation. Social media has blurred the boundaries for leaders. Politicians have always been held accountable for their utterances and scrutinized for their comments that go into an indelible archive. In the age of social media, perceptions are created against political opponents without so much as a thought given to propriety. Leaders earlier did not have the privilege of this anonymity if they wished to run a full-fledged slander campaign against their political adversaries. In the pre-social media era, leaders could not afford to go wrong with their communication strategy. There was no Twitter to turn to the next day, no follow-up comments could be made, no real-time feedback of the previous speech was available for the leader to make corrections soon after.

Today, allegations are hurled without any attribution to authentic sources. In many cases, the politician's PR machinery does it for him. Surrogate pages on Facebook, Twitter and

Instagram as well as WhatsApp forwards are all tools that every political party employs ruthlessly to build their own campaign and demolish the opponent's. Who exactly came up with 'Pappu' for Rahul Gandhi for the first time? Perhaps we will never know, but its originating source, we all know only too well. This casual and spontaneous spring-boarding of monikers by one political party against its opponents helps it land on a premise that has already clicked with a large voter base. When a public image is being built or broken, it depends on whether the propagator or the defender has a stronger social media team. While the 'Pappu' tag has haunted Rahul Gandhi for a good part of his political career, the Congress party's counter for Narendra Modi, 'suit boot ki sarkar', referring to his pricey hologram suit, did not stick for long because Modi was quick to take remedial actions. Some names stick, some don't. The question of their ingenuity is another story for another day.

Voter turnout has progressively increased and the consolidation of ideas on social media has translated into landslide victories. More people thinking alike also means more people making the same choices. Voting figures in the past three decades have gone up 10 percentage points, from hovering at 57–58 per cent in the 1990s to 67.4 per cent in 2019. Today, even as rural–urban migration has displaced a sizeable section of the voting population, voters are only a call away. While the Election Commission, through its publicity, has pushed voters to come out of their houses to cast their ballot, candidates leave no stone unturned to ensure their supporters travel back home during elections to vote for them. Technology has spared no one, not even a reluctant voter.

It has, however, positively ensured better monitoring, accuracy and faster counting of votes and safekeeping of the electronic voting machines in CCTV-monitored strongrooms. Gone are the days of booth capturing that, possibly at a hyperlocal level, upset what could have been a larger national trend. Something we can retrospectively only speculate, and never know for sure.

Add to this the gradual demographic shift to a larger younger population that is impacted by social media and technology advancement. If in 2001, there were 21 crore eligible voters in the age group of 18–29, this figure went up to 30 crore in 2019. Voters in the age group of 30–39 increased from 14 crore in 2001 to 22 crore in 2019. The percentage of young voters has seen a steady rise, displacing old preferences in terms of candidates and political parties and outmoded campaign tools and techniques. So, we have more young voters who are out there sharing ideas on social media, evaluating them, propagating them, influencing their contemporaries and sometimes even the older generation, arriving largely at a consensus and delivering thumping majorities.

Social media and 24/7 news channels have invaded the privacy of politicians, putting the spotlight on infighting, blame games and tussles for power within political parties that also end up hurting their own prospects. Social media and 24/7 news channels keep a hawk's eye on the goings-on in a politician's life, relaying the nitty-gritties to an ever-inquisitive audience. Take the Punjab elections in 2017, for instance. The AAP that appeared poised to get 100 out of the 117 seats ended up with just 20 due to the bitter internal tussle in the party that played out in front of a national audience. The Congress made unexpected gains in the four months leading to the polls, and a dormant Captain Amarinder Singh emerged stronger than ever before with 77 seats in his kitty.

In Uttar Pradesh, the infighting in the SP cost them heavily while the BJP that was trailing in the second position in all pre-poll surveys leapt ahead at the last minute, grabbing over 80 per cent of the seats in the assembly. Both these elections gave clear, sweeping verdicts.

That is not to say that the village elders or dominant castes have lost their sway over their communities, especially in North India. When our survey teams hit the ground, they are invariably told that a final call on which party to back will be taken once the community meetings are held. Jats, Muslims and Dalits across the country exhibit the strongest sense of community when they vote. Communication has come as a boon for them, ensuring homogeneity in their opinion formulation and voting preferences. Earlier, fatwas were issued through *maulvis* (learned scholars or doctors) to consolidate the Muslim vote, but now, smartphones have connected everyone. Victory or loss in most elections is decisive.

For instance, *khaps* (community organizations) in Haryana have a very strong network. They consult among themselves and issue a diktat right before the polls. Earlier, the talks would be held over a mahapanchayat, but now the consensus-building starts much earlier, as khaps reach out to one another over the phone, weigh their options and begin building *mahaul* (public sentiment) for the candidate and party of their choice. In the 2019 Haryana polls, out of 32 Jat-dominated seats, candidates in 24 seats won by a margin of over 10,000 votes, a clear indication that Jat voters made clear choices in favour of a single party despite several Jat candidates in the fray. Interestingly, most seats were bagged either by the Congress or the Jannayak Janata Party (JJP), both led by strong Jat leaders, Bhupinder Singh Hooda and Dushyant Chautala, respectively. On all these seats, the BJP remained in the second spot, in a clear indication that the Jat vote did not get split between the Congress and the JJP. The BJP, led by Manohar Lal Khattar, a non-Jat, managed to grab just seven of the 32 seats. In what would otherwise have been a confusing election, with the JJP, the Indian National Lok Dal (INLD) and the Congress all wooing the same community, voters smartly sifted the best options for themselves on a seat-by-seat basis. They ruled out the INLD and chose the Congress or JJP with extreme clarity. I attribute this maturity solely to a good communication network.

Conversely, in the Lok Sabha elections in 2014 in Mahasamund in Chhattisgarh, local heavyweight and former chief minister Ajit Jogi's strategy to spread misinformation against his contender helped him narrow down the margin. The BJP's Chandu Lal Sahu, who was expected to win by virtue of the 'tsunami' (landslide victory credited to Modi), ended up getting past the line by a thin margin of 1,600 votes, as his opponents propped up 10 namesakes. The other Chandu Lal Sahus ate into the BJP contender's votes, giving Jogi the edge.

A hilarious story from 2003 in Madhya Pradesh comes to mind. In Paraswada constituency, political adversaries of the local heavyweight, Kankar Munjare of the SP, ganged up and fielded a local tribal, Darbu Singh Uikey, against him. Uikey was funded and fuelled to take on Munjare and, in an unexpected turn of events, he ended up defeating Munjare. Uikey, the ragged, barefoot pawn, was so petrified after his victory that he went missing and the divisional magistrate was then tasked to hunt him down. Uikey was dragged back to acknowledge his victory. Poor communication and lack of technology cost some big leaders big heartbreaks for no fault of their own.

All said, the question of who gets elected is baffling in both size and complexity. Elections is not a game for ordinary players. Not everyone gets elected, but those who do are the ones who persist determinedly amidst setbacks, and remain focussed on the larger picture.

~

APPENDIX

AXIS MY INDIA: TRACK RECORD

NUMBER OF ELECTIONS (INCLUDING 2014 AND 2019 GENERAL ELECTIONS)	MOST ACCURATE PREDICTIONS
60	56*

*93 per cent+ accuracy rate

Note: The following data for the election results have been sourced from Election Results Portal, Election Commission of India, https://bit.ly/3KxCLet.

2013 ASSEMBLY ELECTION

MADHYA PRADESH (8 December 2013)—230 Seats			
PARTY	**BJP**	**INC**	**OTHERS**
Axis My India Predictions	162	60	8
Results	**165**	**58**	**7**

CHHATTISGARH (8 December 2013)—90 Seats			
PARTY	**BJP**	**INC**	**OTHERS**
Axis My India Predictions	48	38	4
Results	**49**	**39**	**2**

DELHI (8 December 2013)—70 Seats				
PARTY	**BJP**	**INC**	**AAP**	**OTHERS**
Axis My India Predictions	24	17	27	2
Results	**32**	**8**	**28**	**2**

RAJASTHAN (8 December 2013)—200 Seats			
PARTY	**BJP**	**INC**	**OTHERS**
Axis My India Predictions	106	78	16
Results	**163**	**21**	**16**

2014 ASSEMBLY ELECTION

MAHARASHTRA (19 October 2014)—288 Seats					
PARTY	**BJP**	**SHIV SENA**	**INC**	**NCP**	**OTHERS**
Axis My India Predictions	98–108	84–93	43–48	33–38	15
Results	**122**	**63**	**42**	**41**	**20**

HARYANA (19 October 2014)—90 Seats					
PARTY	**INLD**	**BJP**	**INC**	**HJC (BL)**	**OTHERS**
Axis My India Predictions	31–35	29–33	18–20	3	4
Results	**19**	**47**	**15**	**2**	**7**

JHARKHAND (23 December 2014)—81 Seats						
PARTY	**BJP**	**AJSU**	**INC**	**JVM**	**JMM**	**OTHERS**
Axis My India Predictions	34–38	3–5	4–6	12–16	10–14	7–14
Results	**37**	**5**	**5**	**8**	**19**	**7**

JAMMU AND KASHMIR (23 December 2014)—87 Seats					
PARTY	**PDP**	**BJP**	**INC**	**JKNC**	**OTHERS**
Axis My India Predictions	36–41	16–22	9–13	9–13	6–10
Results	**28**	**25**	**12**	**15**	**7**

2014 GENERAL ELECTION

LOK SABHA ELECTION (16 May 2014)—543 Seats				
PARTY	**NDA**	**UPA**	**LEFT**	**OTHERS**
Axis My India Predictions	287	107	25	124
Results	**336**	**59**	**11**	**137**

2015 ASSEMBLY ELECTION

DELHI (10 February 2015)—70 Seats				
PARTY	**BJP**	**INC**	**AAP**	**OTHERS**
Axis My India Predictions	17±7	0–2	53±7	0
Results	**3**	**0**	**67**	**0**

BIHAR (8 November 2015)—243 Seats			
PARTY	**JD(U)+**	**BJP+**	**OTHERS**
Axis My India Predictions	169–183	58–70	3–7
Results	**178**	**58**	**7**

2016 ASSEMBLY ELECTION

ASSAM (19 May 2016)—126 Seats							
PARTY	**BJP+**	BJP	AGP	BPF	**INC**	**AIUDF**	**OTHERS**
Axis My India Predictions	79–93	56–65	13–16	10–12	26–33	6–10	1–4
Results	86	60	14	12	26	13	1

KERALA (19 May 2016)—140 Seats				
PARTY	**LDF**	**UDF**	**BJP**	**OTHERS**
Axis My India Predictions	88–101	38–48	0–3	1–4
Results	**91**	**47**	**1**	**1**

PUDUCHERRY (19 May 2016)—30 Seats				
PARTY	**INC+DMK**	**AINRC**	**AIADMK**	**OTHERS**
Axis My India Predictions	15–21	8–12	1–4	0–2
Results	**17**	**8**	**4**	**1**

WEST BENGAL (19 May 2016)—294 Seats					
PARTY	**TMC**	**LEFT+INC**	**BJP**	**GOJAM**	**OTHERS**
Axis My India Predictions	233–253	38–51	1–5	3	2
Results	**211**	**76**	**3**	**3**	**1**

TAMIL NADU (19 May 2016)—232/234 Seats				
PARTY	**AIADMK**	**DMK+INC**	**BJP**	**OTHERS**
Axis My India Predictions	89–101	124–140	0–3	4–8
Results	**134**	**98**	**0**	**0**

2017 MUNICIPAL CORPORATION OF DELHI (MCD) ELECTION

MCD OVERALL (26 April 2017)—270 Wards				
PARTY	**AAP**	**BJP**	**INC**	**OTHERS**
Axis My India Predictions	23–35	202–220	19–31	2–8
Results	**48**	**181**	**30**	**11**

EAST DELHI (26 April 2017)—63 Wards				
PARTY	**AAP**	**BJP**	**INC**	**OTHERS**
Axis My India Predictions	6–10	45–51	4–8	0–2
Results	**11**	**47**	**3**	**2**

SOUTH DELHI (26 April 2017)—104 Wards				
PARTY	**AAP**	**BJP**	**INC**	**OTHERS**
Axis My India Predictions	9–13	79–85	7–11	1–3
Results	**16**	**70**	**12**	**6**

NORTH DELHI (26 April 2017)—103 Wards				
PARTY	**AAP**	**BJP**	**INC**	**OTHERS**
Axis My India Predictions	8–12	78–84	8–12	1–3
Results	**21**	**64**	**15**	**3**

2017 MUNICIPAL CORPORATION ELECTION

BRIHANMUMBAI MUNICIPAL CORPORATION (23 February 2017)—227 Wards							
PARTY	**SS**	**BJP+**	**INC**	**NCP**	**MNS**	**SP**	**OTHERS**
Axis My India Predictions	86–92	80–88	30–34	3–6	5–7	2–4	5–7
Results	84	82	31	9	7	5	9

THANE (23 February 2017)—131 Wards					
PARTY	**SS**	**BJP**	**INC**	**NCP**	**OTHERS**
Axis My India Predictions	62–70	26–33	2–6	29–34	0
Results	**67**	**23**	**3**	**34**	**4**

NAGPUR (23 February 2017)—151 Wards					
PARTY	**BJP**	**INC**	**SS**	**BSP**	**OTHERS**
Axis My India Predictions	98–110	35–41	2–4	1–2	3–5
Results	**108**	**29**	**2**	**1**	**11**

PUNE (23 February 2017)—162 Wards					
PARTY	**BJP**	**INC+ NCP**	**SS**	**MNS**	**OTHERS**
Axis My India Predictions	77–85	60–66	10–13	3–6	1–3
Results	**69**	**50**	**10**	**2**	**4**

2017 ASSEMBLY ELECTION

UTTAR PRADESH (11 March 2017)—403 Seats					
PARTY	**BJP+**	**SP+INC**	**BSP**	**RLD**	**OTHERS**
Axis My India Predictions	251–279	88–112	28–42	2–5	4–11
Results	**325**	**54**	**19**	**1**	**4**

UTTARAKHAND (11 March 2017)—70 Seats				
PARTY	**BJP**	**INC**	**BSP**	**OTHERS**
Axis My India Predictions	46–53	12–21	1–2	1–4
Results	**57**	**11**	–	**2**

PUNJAB (11 March 2017)—117 Seats				
PARTY	**AAP**	**INC**	**SAD+BJP**	**OTHERS**
Axis My India Predictions	42–51	62–71	4–7	0–2
Results	**20**	**77**	**18**	**2**

GOA (11 March 2017)—40 Seats					
PARTY	**BJP**	**INC**	**AAP**	**SS+MGP+VL**	**OTHERS**
Axis My India Predictions	18–22	9–13	0–2	3–6	1–3
Results	**13**	**17**	–	**3**	**7**

MANIPUR (11 March 2017)—60 Seats				
PARTY	**INC**	**BJP**	**NPF**	**OTHERS**
Axis My India Predictions	30–36	16–22	3–5	3–6
Results	**28**	**21**	**4**	**7**

GUJARAT (14 December 2017)—182 Seats			
PARTY	**BJP**	**INC+**	**OTHERS**
Axis My India Predictions	99–113	68–82	1–4
Results	**99**	**80**	**3**

HIMACHAL PRADESH (14 December 2017)—68 Seats			
PARTY	**BJP**	**INC+**	**OTHERS**
Axis My India Predictions	47–55	13–20	0–2
Results	**44**	**21**	**3**

2018 ASSEMBLY ELECTION

TRIPURA (3 March 2018)—59 Seats			
PARTY	**BJP**	**LEFT Front**	**OTHERS**
Axis My India Predictions	44–50	9–15	0–3
Results	**43**	**16**	**0**

MEGHALAYA (3 March 2018)—59 Seats								
PARTY	**INC**	**NPP**	**UDP**	**BJP**	**HSPDP**	**PDF**	**NCP**	**IND**
Axis My India Predictions	20	14	6	5	5	3	2	4
Results	**21**	**19**	**6**	**2**	**2**	**4**	**1**	**4**

KARNATAKA (15 May 2018)—222/224 Seats				
PARTY	**INC**	**BJP**	**JD(S)+**	**OTHERS**
Axis My India Predictions	106–118	79–92	22–30	1–4
Results	**78**	**104**	**37**	**3**

MIZORAM (11 December 2018)—40 Seats				
PARTY	**MNF**	**ZPM**	**INC**	**OTHERS**
Axis My India Predictions	16–22	8–12	8–12	1–4
Results	**26**	**8**	**5**	**1**

MADHYA PRADESH (11 December 2018)—230 Seats				
PARTY	**INC**	**BJP**	**BSP**	**OTHERS**
Axis My India Predictions	104–122	102–120	1–3	3–8
Results	**114**	**109**	**2**	**5**

TELANGANA (11 December 2018)—119 Seats					
PARTY	**TRS**	**INC+**	**BJP**	**AMIM**	**OTHERS**
Axis My India Predictions	79–91	21–33	1–3	4–7	0
Results	**88**	**21**	**1**	**7**	**2**

CHHATTISGARH (11 December 2018)—90 Seats				
PARTY	**INC**	**BJP**	**JCC+BSP**	**OTHERS**
Axis My India Predictions	55–65	21–31	4–8	0
Results	**68**	**15**	**7**	**0**

RAJASTHAN (11 December 2018)—199/200 Seats				
PARTY	**INC**	**BJP**	**BSP**	**OTHERS**
Axis My India Predictions	119–141	55–72	1–3	3–8
Results	**101**	**73**	**6**	**19**

2019 ASSEMBLY ELECTION

ANDHRA PRADESH (23 May 2019)—175 Seats						
PARTY	**YSRCP**	**TDP**	**JSP**	**INC**	**BJP**	**OTHERS**
Axis My India Predictions	119–135	39–51	1–3	0	0	0–2
Results	**151**	**23**	**1**	**0**	**0**	**0**

ODISHA (23 May 2019)—146 Seats				
PARTY	**BJD**	**BJP**	**INC**	**OTHERS**
Axis My India Predictions	89–105	29–43	8–12	0–3
Results	**112**	**23**	**9**	**2**

2019 GENERAL ELECTION

(Survey Sample Size—742,187)

Alliance/Party-Wise Seat Share

Alliance	Prediction	Result
BJP+ (NDA)	339–365 (Mid Point: 352)	**352**
INC+ (UPA)	77–108 (Mid Point: 92/93	**92**
OTHERS	69–95	**98**

Party	Prediction	Result
BJP	293–316 (Mid Point: 304)	**303**
INC	48–65 (Mid Point: 56)	**52**

Seat-by-Seat Accuracy: 511 (94 per cent) correct predictions out of 542

Alliance/Party-Wise Vote Share (in Percentage)

Alliance	Party	Party-Wise		Alliance-Wise	
		Prediction	Result	Prediction	Result
BJP+ (NDA)	**BJP**	37	**37.4**	45	**44.8**
	BJP Allies	8	**7.4**		
INC+ (UPA)	**INC**	20	**19.5**	27	**26.8**
	INC Allies	7	**7.3**		
OTHERS	**Regional**	**28**	**28.4**	**28**	**28.4**

2019 GENERAL ELECTION

DAMAN AND DIU	
Axis My India Predictions	**Final Results**
BJP	BJP

LAKSHADWEEP	
Axis My India Predictions	**Final Results**
INC	NCP

PUDUCHERRY	
Axis My India Predictions	**Final Results**
INC	INC

ANDAMAN AND NICOBAR ISLANDS	
Axis My India Predictions	**Final Results**
BJP	INC

CHANDIGARH	
Axis My India Predictions	**Final Results**
BJP	BJP

DADRA AND NAGAR HAVELI	
Axis My India Predictions	**Final Results**
BJP	OTHERS

MIZORAM	
Axis My India Predictions	**Final Results**
ZPM/INC	MNF

NAGALAND	
Axis My India Predictions	**Final Results**
INC	NDPP

TRIPURA—2 SEATS	
Axis My India Predictions	**Final Results**
BJP	BJP
BJP	BJP

SIKKIM	
Axis My India Predictions	**Final Results**
SKM/SDF*	SKM

*A tough fight, where the margin between first two parties is three per cent or less. The party shown first has the edge.

ARUNACHAL PRADESH—2 Seats	
Axis My India Predictions	**Final Results**
BJP	BJP
BJP	BJP

MANIPUR—2 Seats	
Axis My India Predictions	**Final Results**
BJP	BJP
BJP	OTHERS

MEGHALAYA—2 Seats	
Axis My India Predictions	**Final Results**
INC	INC
NPP	NPP

2019 GENERAL ELECTION

JAMMU AND KASHMIR—6 Seats					
PARTY	**BJP**	**INC**	**JKNC**	**PDP**	**OTHERS**
Axis My India Predictions	2–3	0–1	2–3	0	0
Results	**3**	**0**	**3**	**0**	**0**

TAMIL NADU—38/39 Seats*			
PARTY	**BJP+**	**INC+**	**OTHERS**
Axis My India Predictions	0–4	34–38	0
Results	**1**	**37**	**0**

*The Vellore seat election got postponed

TELANGANA—17 Seats					
PARTY	**TRS**	**INC**	**BJP**	**AIMIM**	**OTHERS**
Axis My India Predictions	10–12	1–3	1–3	0–1	0
Results	**9**	**3**	**4**	**1**	**0**

UTTAR PRADESH—80 Seats				
PARTY	**BJP+**	**MGB**	**INC+**	**OTHERS**
Axis My India Predictions	62–68	10–16	1–2	0
Results	**64**	**15**	**1**	**0**

UTTARAKHAND—5 Seats				
PARTY	**BJP**	**INC**	**BSP**	**OTHERS**
Axis My India Predictions	5	0	0	0
Results	**5**	**0**	**0**	**0**

WEST BENGAL—42 Seats					
PARTY	**TMC**	**BJP**	**INC**	**CPM/CPI**	**OTHERS**
Axis My India Predictions	19–22	19–23	0–1	0	0
Results	**22**	**18**	**2**	**0**	**0**

GOA—2 Seats			
PARTY	**BJP**	**INC**	**OTHERS**
Axis My India Predictions	2	0	0
Results	**1**	**1**	**0**

MAHARASHTRA—48 Seats				
PARTY	**BJP+**	**INC+**	**VBA+**	**OTHERS**
Axis My India Predictions	38–42	6–10	0	0
Results	**41**	**6**	**1**	**0**

DELHI—7 Seats				
PARTY	**AAP**	**BJP**	**INC**	**OTHERS**
Axis My India Predictions	0	6–7	0–1	0
Results	**0**	**7**	**0**	**0**

ODISHA—21 Seats				
PARTY	**BJD**	**BJP**	**INC**	**OTHERS**
Axis My India Predictions	2–6	15–19	0–1	0
Results	**12**	**8**	**1**	**0**

PUNJAB—13 Seats				
PARTY	**BJP+**	**INC**	**AAP**	**OTHERS**
Axis My India Predictions	3–5	8–9	0–1	0
Results	**4**	**8**	**1**	**0**

RAJASTHAN—25 Seats			
PARTY	**BJP+**	**INC**	**OTHERS**
Axis My India Predictions	23–25	0–2	0
Results	**25**	**0**	**0**

HIMACHAL PRADESH—4 Seats			
PARTY	**BJP+**	**INC**	**OTHERS**
Axis My India Predictions	4	0	0
Results	**4**	**0**	**0**

JHARKHAND—14 Seats			
PARTY	**BJP+**	**INC+**	**OTHERS**
Axis My India Predictions	12–14	0–2	0
Results	**12**	**2**	**0**

KARNATAKA—28 Seats			
PARTY	**BJP**	**INC+**	**OTHERS**
Axis My India Predictions	21–25	3–6	0–1
Results	**25**	**2**	**1**

KERALA—20 Seats				
PARTY	**UDF (INC)**	**LDF**	**NDA**	**OTHERS**
Axis My India Predictions	15–16	3–5	0–1	0
Results	**19**	**1**	**0**	**0**

MADHYA PRADESH—29 Seats			
PARTY	**BJP**	**INC**	**OTHERS**
Axis My India Predictions	26–28	1–3	0
Results	**28**	**1**	**0**

ANDHRA PRADESH—25 Seats						
PARTY	**YSRCP**	**TDP**	**JSP**	**INC**	**BJP**	**OTHERS**
Axis My India Predictions	18–20	4–6	0–1	0	0	0
Results	**22**	**3**	**0**	**0**	**0**	**0**

ASSAM—14 Seats				
PARTY	**BJP+**	**INC**	**AIUDF**	**OTHERS**
Axis My India Predictions	12–14	0–2	0	0
Results	**9**	**3**	**1**	**1**

BIHAR—40 Seats			
PARTY	**BJP+**	**INC**	**OTHERS**
Axis My India Predictions	38–40	0–2	0
Results	**39**	**1**	**0**

CHHATTISGARH—11 Seats			
PARTY	**BJP**	**INC**	**OTHERS**
Axis My India Predictions	7–8	3–4	0–1
Results	**9**	**2**	**0**

GUJARAT—26 Seats			
PARTY	**BJP**	**INC**	**OTHERS**
Axis My India Predictions	25–26	0–1	0
Results	**26**	**0**	**0**

HARYANA—10 Seats					
PARTY	**BJP**	**INC**	**AAP+JJP**	**INLD**	**OTHERS**
Axis My India Predictions	8–10	0–2	0	0	0
Results	**10**	**0**	**0**	**0**	**0**

2019 ASSEMBLY ELECTION

JHARKHAND (21 December 2019)—81 Seats					
PARTY	**BJP**	**AJSU**	**INC+JMM+RJD**	**JVM**	**OTHERS**
Axis My India Predictions	22–32	3–5	38–50	2–4	4–7
Results	**25**	**2**	**47**	**3**	**4**

MAHARASHTRA (24 October 2019)—288 Seats				
PARTY	**BJP+SHIV SENA**	**INC+NCP**	**VBA**	**OTHERS***
Axis My India Predictions	166–194	72–90	0–2	22–32
Results	**161**	**98**	**0**	**29**

**Others*: AIMIM, BVA, CPIM, SP, PWPI, PJP, MNS, JSS, KSP, RSP, SWP, SBP and Independents

Note: Wherever a description of Others is given, it includes small parties and Independents. Where a description is not given of Others, it is only Independents.

HARYANA (24 October 2019)—90 Seats				
PARTY	**BJP**	**INC**	**JJP**	**OTHERS***
Axis My India Predictions	32–44	30–42	6–10	6–10
Results	**40**	**31**	**10**	**9**

**Others*: HLP/INLD and Independents

2020 ASSEMBLY ELECTION

DELHI (11 February 2020)—70 Seats				
PARTY	**AAP**	**BJP+**	**INC+**	**OTHERS**
Axis My India Predictions	59–68	2–11	0	0
Results	**62**	**8**	**0**	**0**

BIHAR (10 November 2020)—243 Seats						
PARTY	**NDA**	**MGB**	**LJP**	**GDSF**	**PDA**	**OTHERS**
Axis My India Predictions	69–91	139–161	3–5	3–5	0	3–5
Results	**125**	**110**	**1**	**6**	**0**	**1**

NDA: BJP, JDU, VIP and HAM

MGB: RJD, INC, CPI(ML)L, CPI and CPI(M)

2021 ASSEMBLY ELECTION

ASSAM (2 May 2021)—126 Seats			
PARTY	**BJP+**	**INC+**	**OTHERS**
Axis My India Predictions	75–85	40–50	0–2
Results	**75**	**50**	**1**

KERALA (2 May 2021)—140 Seats				
PARTY	**UDF**	**LDF**	**NDA**	**OTHERS**
Axis My India Predictions	20–36	104–120	0–2	0–2
Results	**41**	**99**	**0**	**0**

PUDUCHERRY (2 May 2021)—30 Seats			
PARTY	**NDA**	**UPA**	**OTHERS**
Axis My India Predictions	20–24	6–10	0–1
Results	**16 + 4***	**9**	**1**

*Friendly fight of AINRC (3) and AIADMK (1) candidates as Independent won

TAMIL NADU (2 May 2021)—234 Seats						
PARTY	**AIADMK+**	**DMK+**	**AMMK+**	**MNM+**	**NTK+**	**OTHERS**
Axis My India Predictions	38–54	175–195	1–2	0–2	0–2	0–1
Results	**75**	**159**	**0**	**0**	**0**	**0**

WEST BENGAL (2 May 2021)—292/294 Seats*				
PARTY	**BJP+**	**TMC+**	**LEFT+**	**OTHERS**
Axis My India Predictions	134–160	130–156	0–2	0–1
Results	77	214	1 (RSMP)	0

*The election for two seats got postponed

2022 ASSEMBLY ELECTION

UTTAR PRADESH (10 March 2022)—403 Seats					
PARTY	**BJP+**	**SP+**	**BSP**	**INC**	**OTHERS**
Axis My India Predictions	288–326	71–101	3–9	1–3	2–3
Results	**273**	**125**	**1**	**2**	**2**

PUNJAB (10 March 2022)—117 Seats					
PARTY	**AAP**	**INC**	**SAD+**	**BJP+**	**OTHERS**
Axis My India Predictions	76–90	19–31	7–11	1–4	0–2
Results	**92**	**18**	**4**	**2**	**1**

UTTARAKHAND (10 March 2022)—70 Seats				
PARTY	**BJP**	**INC**	**BSP**	**OTHERS**
Axis My India Predictions	36–46	20–30	2–4	2–5
Results	**47**	**19**	**2**	**2**

MANIPUR (10 March 2022)—60 Seats						
PARTY	**BJP**	**INC+**	**NPP**	**NPF**	**JD(U)**	**OTHERS**
Axis My India Predictions	33–43	4–8	4–8	4–8	2–4	0–3
Results	**32**	**5**	**7**	**5**	**6**	**5**

GOA (10 March 2022)—40 Seats				
PARTY	**BJP**	**INC+**	**MGP+TMC**	**OTHERS**
Axis My India Predictions	14–18	15–20	2–5	0–4
Results	**20**	**12**	**2**	**6**

HIMACHAL PRADESH (8 December 2022)—68 Seats				
PARTY	**BJP**	**INC**	**AAP**	**OTHERS***
Axis My India Predictions	24–34	30–40	0	4–8
Results	**25**	**40**	**0**	**3**

**Others*: BSP, RDP, CPM/CPI and IND

GUJARAT (8 December 2022)—182 Seats				
PARTY	**BJP**	**INC**	**AAP**	**OTHERS***
Axis My India Predictions	129–151	16–30	9–21 (single digit)**	2–6
Results	**156**	**17**	**5**	**4**

**Others*: BTP, AIMIM, NCP, IND, etc.

**The next day's exit poll prediction was revised—'AAP seat share to be in single digits, and AAP vote share from 20% to 15%.'

MCD (7 December 2022)—250 Wards				
PARTY	**AAP**	**BJP**	**INC**	**OTHERS***
Axis My India Predictions	149–171	69–91	3–7	5–9
Results	**134**	**104**	**9**	**3**

**Others*: BSP, NCP, JD(U), AIMIM, IND, etc.

2023 ASSEMBLY ELECTION

NAGALAND (2 March 2023)—60 Seats								
PARTY	**NDPP + BJP**	**INC**	**NPF**	**NCP**	**LJP**	**RPI (A)**	**NPP**	**OTHERS***
Axis My India Predictions	38–48	1–2	3–8	4–8	1–3	0–2	0–2	1–5
RESULTS	**37**	**0**	**2**	**7**	**2**	**2**	**5**	**5**

*Others: JDU, IND, RLD and RPP

MEGHALAYA (2 March 2023)—59/60 Seats*						
PARTY	**NPP**	**INC**	**TMC**	**BJP**	**UDP**	**OTHERS****
Axis My India Predictions	18–24	6–12	5–9	4–8	8–12	4–8
RESULTS	**26**	**5**	**5**	**2**	**11**	**10**

*Election postponed for Sohiong (Assembly Constituency 23)
**Others: VPP, HSPDP, PDF, GNC, RPI(A), JD(U), GSP and Independents

TRIPURA (2 March 2023)—60 Seats				
PARTY	**BJP+IPFT**	**LEFT FRONT+INC***	**TIPRA MOTHA**	**OTHERS****
Axis My India Predictions	36–45	6–11	9–16	0
RESULTS	**33**	**14**	**13**	**0**

*Alliance partner for Left Front: CPM/Congress/CPI/RSP/AIFB/IND
**Others: TMC, IND, RPI(A), Tripura Peoples Party and Nationalist Citizens Party of India

INDEX